TOWARD A
MARXIST PSYCHOLOGY

BY THE SAME AUTHOR

Radical Psychology
  EDITED BY PHIL BROWN

Toward a Marxist Psychology

Phil Brown

HARPER COLOPHON BOOKS
Harper & Row, Publishers
New York, Evanston,
San Francisco, London

TOWARD A MARXIST PSYCHOLOGY

Copyright © 1974 by Philip M. Brown

First HARPER COLOPHON edition published 1974

LIBRARY OF CONGRESS CATALOG CARD NUMBER: 73–17853

STANDARD BOOK NUMBER: 06–091012–7

To Becky Tippens

Contents

Acknowledgments

Writing the final draft of this book was a wonderful experience. Friends' help extended beyond simply reading and criticizing the manuscript; discussions about, which reached into personal and political areas, quite transformed the book. Becky Tippens was incredibly helpful, reading the manuscript and giving important criticisms and suggestions. She helped me to clarify some overall relationships of psychology to politics, as well as to expand the scope of the material. Particularly in the areas of sexuality, family structure, and Wilhelm Reich, Becky helped me to understand their psychological appearances in a clearer framework of politics. Richard Krushnic read large parts of the manuscript and offered helpful suggestions, at times in discussion with Becky and myself. Karen Rotkin helped out on the sexuality chapter. My courses at the Cambridge-Goddard Graduate School were also helpful in that my students continually aided me in clarifying many thoughts. Cynthia

Merman, my editor, has again been wonderful at every step. Thank you all.

Toward a Marxist Psychology represents much of the last five years of my life, mostly as a political activist in the amorphous thing we call the Movement. If there is a way to acknowledge that, I hope the book's usefulness will be it.

Prelude: After Artaud on Van Gogh

Artaud wrote "Van Gogh: The Man Suicided by Society" as a reflection of his own understanding of what was being done to him. Surrealist radical committed to be crazy since crazy was the enemy. Artaud, freaked by the straight world, and struggling for a new one, felt that he and Van Gogh and their kind (our kind?) were geniuses, persecuted for that.

> "Thus it is that a tainted society invented psychiatry to defend itself against the investigations of certain superior lucidities whose faculties of divinations troubled it.[1]

Society freaked because there were superior lucidities—in the possibility of every person's life. And living.

> No. Van Gogh was not mad, but his paintings were flamethrowers, atomic bombs, whose angles of vision,

[1] Antonin Artaud, "Van Gogh: The Man Suicided by Society" in Jack Hirschner, ed., *Artaud Anthology* (San Francisco: San Francisco City Lights Books, 1965). All subsequent quotations are from the same source.

compared to all the other painting that was going strong at the time, would have been capable of seriously disturbing the larval conformism of the Second Empire bourgeoisie and the myrmidons of Thiers, Gambetta, Felix Faure, as well as those of Napoleon the Third.

It is the destruction of the lucidity in all—not just Van Gogh—that creates our first awareness of the psychiatric empire.

Compared to Van Gogh's lucidity, which keeps working away, psychiatry is nothing but a den of gorillas, themselves obsessed and persecuted, which, to palliate the most frightful states of human anguish and suffocation, have merely a ridiculous terminology.

But it's clearly more than terminology. It's the school psychologist visiting the parents and asking why their fourth grade child drinks coffee. It's the adjustment of the lonely housewives and tired-out civil service clerks, secure in their self-fulfilled nothingness put upon them by paperback psychology books.

Psychiatry is born of the vulgar rabble of creatures who have wanted to preserve the evil at the source of the illness and who have rooted out of their own nothingness a kind of Swiss guard in order to sap at its base the justifiably rebellious drive which is at the origin of genius.

Rabble-faced, rabble-roused psychiatry—tumbling lunatics to the dungeons. And we don't even know what a lunatic is, other than a defined, role-given wretched human being, wailing while no one hears, or even thinks there is anything to hear. Utterances and howls are intelligible, even if wrong.

Talented, untalented. Breathe life, then revolt. Shrinks in *Fahrenheit 451* trucks burning out your brains. And then, they are actually affronted when reproached. Lobotomies are back, you can read it in the journals.

> I too am like poor Van Gogh, I no longer think, but
> every day I manage more and more finely terrific in-
> ternal turmoils and I would like to see any doctor come
> and reproach me for tiring myself.

Tiring oneself to prevent them from doing it to you, or
tiring yourself in your project. If it's your project, it's
no good.

> And there was between Dr. Gachet and Van Gogh's
> brother Thee any number of those stinking family con-
> fabulations with directors of insane asylums regarding
> the *patient* whom they had brought to them.

Painting was Van Gogh's weapon, so say Artaud and
others, and many others. Our weapons are often dis-
guised, but known to us in the recesses of our heads
where the dreams of freedom often tell us what to do.

> Whoever doesn't smell of cooked bomb and com-
> pressed vertigo is not worthy of being alive.

But then again, it's not a question of worth, but the
actual functioning and existence. We *do* smell like
that. Laing asked who was crazier, the person claiming to have the bomb inside her/himself, or the person
with the real power to drop that bomb. We continue
to smell like that. The bomb is inside us and revolves
in our bodies as in some cleansed atmosphere ready
for the introduction of a foreign element, an inert gas.

> Besides, one does not commit suicide by oneself.
>   No one was ever born by himself.
>   Nor has anyone died by himself.
>   But in the case of suicide, there has to be an army
> of evil being to impel the body to the unnatural gesture,
> to deny itself its own life.

No glorification of the self-death, for there was no self-
death. No noble savage schizophrenics running
through midtowns of midcentury cities. We are all in
question.

Preface

A rebellious prisoner is given a lobotomy, a "hyper-active" elementary school student is drugged with Ritalin, a sixteen-year-old girl is hospitalized for engaging in sexual relations, a worker dissatisfied with the monotony of an assembly line is given a quick series of electroshock-therapy treatments so that he may return to work, a vice-president of a major corporation is introduced into a sensitivity training group so that he and his corporation may function better.

Psychologists and psychiatrists do these things.

Attica rebels are shot by state troopers, school corridors are patrolled by gun-wielding cops, youths go to jail for their sexual activity, workers are beaten and killed for organizing for their rights, important corporation executives buy off senators so that they will pass a bill guaranteeing higher profits while the masses of United States citizens "eat less."

Capitalists and their agents do these things.

There are no significant differences between these

two groups of activities. The mental health professional and the business manager perform the same functions, although by means of slightly different methods, for they both serve the needs of modern capitalism. This capitalist system is a total organization of human existence: it incorporates economic oppression, social organization, "popular" culture, ethics and morality, interpersonal relations, and everything else. It is a system that takes humanity away from the earth that has created it and from the world that humanity has created.

As American capitalism develops, it takes on new and subtler forms in addition to brute force. The mental health industry is one of these forms. While the psychologists, psychiatrists, and allied professionals have become overtly more brutal in recent years, the bulk of their work is concerned with covert methods of social control.

This book is concerned with exploring the integral relationship between the psychology racket and the capitalist monster. I am writing it not as an academic exercise but as a political practice that comes from my theory and my action, the goal of which is human liberation through a socialist revolution that will integrate political and personal freedom. More important, it comes from the theory and practice of countless comrades in this country and throughout the world.

I draw lines between friends and enemies, since that is a clear necessity. I don't aim to compartmentalize the world, though, or to take a pessimistic view of human liberation. The struggles we all face are struggles in which we can grow as people while building a new society, and in that I see a great optimism. The majority of people are in opposition to a small minority, and the differences between the masses of people are beginning to be resolved.

In attempting to work out a Marxist psychology, I am taking a step that may seem precipitous, but I don't offer this up as dogma. It is an approach, and it will require change—I expect that and look forward to it.

Above all, this book seeks to contribute to a theory and practice of revolution. The initial critique is always necessary, but we must move ahead with our struggle.

Introduction:
What Is the Problem?

Psychology is more than just a professional field of work. It is also a codified ideology and practice that arises from the nature of our capitalist society and functions to bolster that society. Although some of the work of professional psychology and psychiatry is quite overtly oppressive (witness the rise of psychosurgery, electroshock, and behavior modification for rebellious prisoners), the bulk of psychological manipulation is covert. Hidden below the surface platitudes of social science, industrial psychologists join with the state hospitals in disciplining the working class, creating various devices to stifle popular recognition of oppression and subsequent revolutionary action. This book will be concerned with presenting and explaining the atrocities of the psychiatric and psychological professions and their part in the class rule of the United States, and with methods for ending that class rule.

The first things that come to most people's minds when they hear the word "psychology" are mental health, therapy, psychiatric hospitals. True, these are major parts of psychology but not its whole nature. The social control functions of "mental illness" are but a part of the total work of psychology. This is particularly true when we see the phenomenon of the state hospital as a repository for primarily working-class people, when we see the psychological abuses in the prison system, and when we observe the racism and sexism of the mental health industry.

Further, the number of workers in the mental health industry is growing all the time. These people make up a considerable portion of the work force in certain areas (Boston is a prime example). Aides, attendants, and lower-level nurses receive the same treatment at their bosses' hands as do workers in factories, department stores, offices, and elsewhere. As with medical workers, mental health workers suffer from being charged with "helping" patients. The fundamental contradiction between administrators' and workers' definitions of "helping" divides these workers from their patients.

The differences between mental hospitals and prisons are breaking down. On the one hand, the "decentralization" of mental health facilities implies the need on the rulers' part for more "effective" methods of dealing with those persons who do not seem to require placement in a traditional mental hospital. So there is the attempt to close large state hospitals and place people in "community oriented" treatment facilities. Why will this be more effective? Because the abuses of state hospitals are becoming clearer and clearer, and patient and worker unrest can be destroyed by ending the large centralized institution. Additionally, the community mental health center movement has grown to the point where it more effectively cools people out in their neighborhoods.

On the other hand, the terror tactics learned in mental hospitals are now being used in prisons. Lobotomies (and other forms of psychosurgery) are on a sharp increase, as are behavior modification/ brainwashing techniques (in the manner of *1984* and *A Clockwork Orange*).[1] It is no accident that the prime candidates for psychosurgery and behavior modification are those prisoners whose politics and sexuality are not in accord with socially accepted norms. Prison administrators have learned that simply detaining "criminals" will not wipe out their "antisocial" behavior—mental hospital administrators have known this all along and have thus been enforcing morality and the American way of life on their inmates.

Similar psychological programs are underway in schools. "Hyperactive" students are drugged with Ritalin, and some are even lobotomized. Children who "act out" are subjected to behavior modification programs, which are being sold to school districts by think tanks and psychological consulting firms. The old methods of the school psychologists and guidance counselors—tracking, special schools, etc.—are being modified with more severe, overtly fascist actions. School psychology is important in that it attempts to integrate family training, school indoctrination, and psychological techniques to create passive citizens. A

[1] For a survey of behavior modification and psychosurgery in prisons, see "Check Out Your Mind," *Rough Times*, vol. 3, no. 5. Edited from an article in the Chicago chapter of the National Lawyers Guild paper, *Up against the Bench*, vol. 2, no. 2, this article cites many other articles in *RT* and elsewhere on this subject.

recent series of teachers' seminars, cosponsored by the Norfolk (Massachusetts) Mental Health Association and the Norfolk County Teachers' Association, featured sessions on such topics as "Masturbation: Can a Simple Pleasure Lead to a Complex Problem?" and "How the Detention Period Can Become a Meaningful Therapeutic Hour." What we must ask is: will detention period become psychosurgery period?

In times of student rebellion school psychologists are called upon to aid in the suppression of the young rebels. Police powers are utilized, but because psychologists and counselors are the repressors, it is considered "therapy."[2] Will the "special schools" become youths' versions of California's Vacaville Adjustment Center and the other state and federal facilities for behavior modification? The lines are drawing closer. It has not been difficult for the ruling class to kill striking workers, rebellious prisoners, and student activists in the past. As the times become more troubled, the various actions of the police state occur at higher levels of sophistication.

Industrial and personnel psychologists work on another end of the problem—the point of production.[3] Their goal is to create environments and programs to cool out the workers while securing smoother operation and higher profits for the bosses. After World War I the United States emerged as the world's leading power. Frederick Taylor's industrial efficiency

[2] Dick Moore, "See the Psychologist Run: A School Psychologist's Appraisal of the Efforts of the Bureau of Child Guidance in New York City's Schools," pamphlet of Psychologists for a Democratic Society (August 1969), speaks to this point.

[3] Loren Baritz, *The Servants of Power* (Middletown, Conn.: Wesleyan University Press, 1960) is an excellent survey of applied social science in industry.

movement was an attempt to rationalize and to smooth out the forces of production that had grown to such great proportions at that time. Taylorism was allied, both ideologically and in practice, with the new science of applied psychology. With government funding and support, these allies began to create a technological approach to the production of wealth and the alienation of labor involved in that production. Psychologists working in the factories and elsewhere (large chain stores, etc.) today play an integral role in speedups, selective hiring, and the quelling of workers' insurgency.

The capitalists' need for social science planning arises out of the twentieth-century capitalist approach to work-life discipline. In order to have a relatively stable society with a minimum of class struggle, the forces of a capitalist society inevitably lead to attempts at total discipline. Thus the family, religion, ethics, sexuality, work relations, and so forth, all reflect the separation of work from other parts of life.[4] While the workers are being routinized and codified by industrial psychologists, other psychologists are organizing sensitivity training sessions for executives so that they will not "flip out" in the face of the crazed human technology with which they must deal day after day. They are taught to have no emotions concerning the suppression of workers, planned unemployment, and the like, but are urged to feel self-fulfilled in their managerial functions and in their supposedly individually creative lives.

[4] On the separation of work and life, see Eli Zaretsky, "Capitalism and Personal Life," *Socialist Revolution,* no. 13–14 (January–April 1973). Zaretsky shows the changing nature of work and the family through the class history of the last few centuries, touching on the totality of discipline in capitalist social relations.

Advertising psychologists work in the consumption-distribution area. They design methods of selling goods and services to the masses of people. A large proportion of these goods and services are useless in the sense that they will not create better lives for the users—they in fact perpetuate unknowing subservience to the system—but in the daily struggle for existence, people find themselves hard put to know what is really useful. Since alienated labor yields alienated relations to the products of labor, the advertising psychologists can pervert real needs, altering them into felt needs that typically offer pseudogratification of sexuality, power, individuality, etc., to the purchaser. The TV and magazine ads that we often find sickening are the products of psychologists who have learned to use the alienated desires of people as a means of enforcing distribution. Additionally, this enforced distribution insures not only economic flow but also psychological subservience to a specific alienated life created by capitalist economies.

Social psychologists and experimental psychologists are close to the laboratory situation, seemingly concerned only with research and publication. Actually, the experimentalist who plays with rats is often involved in designing social control programs or pushing a fascist anthropology that analogizes human behavior to the behavior of trapped, mutilated animals. The social psychologist deals in the same experimental model but focuses on devising "empirical" analyses of human behavior. On the benign side, this involves countless experiments and articles to prove truisms such as "the difference between a leader and a follower is that the leader tends to exert pressure on the follower, who in turn tends to accept the pressure of the leader." This is actually not so benign, since in this example it obscures the actual bases of leadership and power by use of a social science model, taking it as a given. On the malignant end social psychologists are integral architects of the major counterinsurgency tactics used in Southeast Asia and elsewhere in the Third World. They work in places like the War (Defense) Department, the C.I.A., the Hudson Institute, and our major universities.

The mental health and psychology professionals have projected an ideology that derives from the class basis of capitalism. It is inevitable that the unfree relations of our daily lives would be codified and exploited by these professionals who are in the employment of the ruling class or in the ideological support network of ruling-class institutions. It is not at all surprising that blacks and women receive the same treatment from psychologists as they do from government and corporate officials. The prevailing racism and sexism in the psychology fields is usually quite overt. The reader will notice such attitudes, and criticisms of them, throughout this book, although I have chosen not to attempt a separate analysis of racism and sexism in psychology and psychiatry. The Bibliography at the end of the book lists some necessary reading. No real understanding of the institutionalized sexism in mental health is possible without Phyllis Chesler's *Women and Madness;* a similar book on racism is yet to arrive, although Thomas and Sillen's *Racism and Psychiatry* is a beginning.

Throughout this book I take a class perspective, which understands the reality of class conflict in capitalist society and relates how the psychologists and psychiatrists—and their institutional framework—attempt to keep the masses of people, working people, in subservience and powerlessness. I keep in mind always the ultimate goal of communism, the abolition of class society—a task that only the "last class," the proletariat (in its broadest sense), can perform.

In fact, what unites the institutions and practitioners of psychology and psychiatry is their role of service to the ruling class. They verbalize the ideology, and perform the duties, of capitalist relations. Too often organized psychology verbally peddles an ideology of benevolent neutrality while in reality it performs functions of class warfare. Its practitioners deal in the dominant ideas and actions of the dominant class and couch them in terms of social science.

The things we call psychology pervade all aspects of existence in our society, since the refinements of total capitalist discipline are refinements touching on the most personal aspects of our lives. Uncovering the mystified and alienated reality of our lives is tied up with discovering the mythology and alienation which psychology expects us to take for granted. Struggle against institutional psychology and psychiatry has become integral to the total struggle for liberation. Further, the demystification of "psychological truth" causes us to see more possibilities of free human existence, to fuse socialist economic organization with the types of free relationships to which it leads.

Alternatives to capitalism seem to be communism, barbarism, or a welfare state—technocracy. Of the three, communism seems to be the inevitable choice, for the working class brought into existence by capitalism can abolish itself and all other classes. In fact, the working people have been creating our world for centuries—it is now a matter of taking over and recreating. To do this we need to know the real enemy, to realize that we, our family, the blacks at work, the hippies, are not the enemy. Once we know that we are not our own enemies, we then know we can all create the new world together.

NOTES ON THE ORDER OF THE BOOK

The order in which I have chosen to develop my views is a carefully constructed one but by no means the only one possible. "Scientism or Dialectics?" is an exposition of the differences between the Western and dialectical ways of looking at the world. This chapter introduces the use of Marxism as a method for life in general and for psychology in particular. I show in this chapter that the ways in which we have learned to think are not natural developments but ways which reinforce our unfreedom.

"The Medical Model" applies Marxism to an exploration of the ideology of mental illness, incorporating the important work of Thomas Szasz, Erving Goffman, and Thomas Scheff. This is a partial step in the overall development, important in its ability to show certain initial critiques of the uses of psychiatric power. The ideas in this chapter lead naturally to more severe questioning of the actual bases of psychiatric power.

"The Freud Problem" locates the importance of criticizing Freudianism, which plays a similar role to the institutionalized psychology dealt with in the previous chapter. I show the pervasive aspects of Freudian thought, placing them historically in the development of modern capitalism. I also point out how the current vogue of a Marx-Freud synthesis is impossible.

Going a step beyond Freudianism, "Wilhelm Reich and the Sexual-Political Struggle" explains the importance of one of Marxism's most insightful interpreters.

The current understanding of Reich by many radicals and socialists is integrally related to new forms of political expression, as exemplified by certain parts of the women's movement. I show how Reich was the first Marxist to begin realizing the unity of political and personal revolution.

"Frantz Fanon: Psychiatry and Revolution" is almost an interlude, presenting the thought of a revolutionary who offers us so much for gaining an understanding of the psychological manifestations of political-economic oppression.

"Antipsychiatry" critically analyzes the movement that has been of prime importance in transcending bourgeois psychology and in leading us to a fuller grasp of the internal dynamics of life under capitalism. As a widespread school of thought with so many different interpretations, antipsychiatry needs to be clarified so that we can extract its valuable kernels.

"Beyond Therapy" deals with some aspects of therapy as a power relationship. This chapter also explores certain countertherapy possibilities that arise from the theory of the preceding chapters.

"Toward Sexual Integration" also evolves a practical nature from the preceding chapters. It offers some views of the sexual captivity that is fundamentally related to our total captivity, utilizing a somewhat Reichian outlook.

"Dare to Struggle, Dare to Win!" attempts to summarize the ideas that have come before, locating them in the context of the total revolution.

The Bibliography lists those books that have been the most helpful to me in creating this book.

1. Scientism or Dialectics?

DOES WESTERN THOUGHT THINK?

One reason why we often cannot clearly see the world around us is that we have been taught to think in certain ways that make reality imperceptible. Our trained, "logical" minds filter out real phenomena in the world and leave us with neat categories that explain away rather than clarify. Also, Western logic counterposes itself to emotions, separating thought and feeling into compartments that rarely interrelate. As R. D. Laing shows, we have mystified experience and are alienated from our behavior, since that behavior comes from an alienated view of the world.

The major tradition of Western thought is "logical." In its present development such logical thought posits certain absolute realities that are at variance with the real world. For instance, Aristotelian logic tells us that we can never have the mutual existence of opposites. Feudal Catholic Europe turned this into a religious dualism, a knowledge privy to aristocrats and clergy. For the majority of people—the serfs—little thought was expected, only obedience to the simplistic transmission of religious dualism by the priests. The development of capitalism brought with it more knowledge, especially when newspapers and magazines began to reach large numbers of people. Tied to this is the development of public education and changes in the family, causing the family to teach the mores and ethics of the dominant class.

Capitalism's striving to master the world in a "rational" way led to "scientific method," that system of thought that is embodied in the introduction to the typical high school science text. It claims that through building up facts that are scientifically repeatable, we can arrive at a theory that will then predict further events. This empiricism destroys the validity of human sensory experience, translating real phenomena into scientific categories. Certain theories become enthroned and are considered unchallengeable, very similar to the church's restrictions on science, except that in capitalist society science replaces religion to the extent of being the moral safeguard of "acceptable" knowledge.

Scientism places this empirical view of the world in a position of absolute truth. It claims that science is value-free, without any social, political, or ethical bias. Thus nuclear scientists claim "pure science" even as Hiroshima and Nagasaki burn; the Harvard sociologist proclaims "pure research" as his work turns into pacification techniques in Vietnam; the research psychologist speaks of "value-free" science as his proof of black inferiority is used to end special education programs for black ghetto youths.

Compartmentalization of knowledge is another cornerstone of the scientific approach to reality. Since reality for the absolute empiricist is a given, there is no reason why the world cannot be divided up into compartments that will each hold a certain delegated amount of knowledge. This knowledge develops into de facto authority as professional associations grow and professional journals multiply. As a result we have "sociology," which cannot answer the questions of "psychology," which cannot answer the questions of "anthropology"—a domain to each.

The absolute reality of the world, as mentioned above, is a conception giving a whole world view to scientific observers. Whether a person is officially of the "positivist" school or not, the positivist view of the world remains his/her basic outlook. In this view the world is an outside reality with definite structures and boundaries. People and the world don't influence each other; nothing is changeable. In such a framework history becomes irrelevant and today's knowledge is considered the ultimate truth.

Now, some knowledge is "true" and other is "false." For example, "the universe revolves around the earth" is generally considered to be false, and "the earth is a small part of the universe, and the earth revolves around the sun" is considered to be true. Most rational people today believe this. Until Copernicus and Galileo, however, equally rational people held different views. What occurred to change this was (1) the world view of the time created the mind that conceived of the new astronomy and (2) scientists found that a new astronomy gave better answers to their questions. It took the development of history to bring about the development of observations of the world. Let us take a short historical look at scientific cornerstones.

In the medieval period the universe was conceived

of as very tangible and earth-centered. Besides being the center of the universe, the earth was the physical center of "spheres," concentrically going outward until the final "empyrean" sphere of heaven. The church sanctified this view, and it fit into the feudal system. With the rise of capitalism and the new outlook on the world, Newtonian physics and the Copernican universe gave birth to the science of reality: a more dynamic world required a more dynamic theory. As capitalism progressed to its modern stage of monopolism and created more alienated and fragmented social relations, quantum physics and relativity came to the fore. I do not list these historical-scientific correlates to imply that they are all figments of the imagination, stemming simply from ideological considerations; rather, the implication is that a "true" fact is something that demands a certain world view to discover it.

Psychology fits into the same pattern. As Freud's sexual determinism provided the reality for Victorian-inherited values, modern social psychologists studying attitude-change discovered how to convince people that student revolutionaries are "mentally ill." This all fits into what the society demands—often it is far less conspiratorial than it seems, yet it mirrors the values of the dominant class.[1] Of course, we know that Freudian metaphysics are wrong, but only in that they stand for *fact;* the Freudian world view is a real response to social conditions and must be understood as

[1] Antonio Gramsci is most important in understanding this relation. Founder of the Italian Communist Party and a major Marxist theoretician, Gramsci's ideas of "cultural hegemony" trace the development of ideology as reflection of dominant class values. See *The Modern Prince and Other Writings* and *Prison Notebooks* (New York: International Publishers, 1969 and 1971).

such. Psychoanalysis grew out of the bourgeois response to material conditions at the end of the century, among them the rising threat of imperialism, workers' movements, familial changes (especially the conflict between bourgeois Victorian purism and proletarian Victorian sexual exploration), and the general changes in capitalist views of human nature. While psychoanalysis was at odds with the empirical psychology of Wilhelm Wundt and others, nevertheless it put forth a scientific position that could be used to explain biologically innate behavior. Such a static view of humanity was part of the increasing total discipline of the work force, especially in that it was the first major antisexual code since that of the Catholic Church. In the same way, today's responsiveness to the area of attitude change is a reflection of the times—if revolution were not a threat, there would be no psychologists studying it, especially in such a thorough manner.

MARXISM AS A METHOD

The validity of Marxism as a method for understanding the world is the next logical step. It is this method that points to the historical correlates discussed earlier and that illuminates reality as defined by the material world around it. History is the continual factor, itself composed of nature, human beings, and the social relations of human beings. Determined at its base by the economic matters of survival, history changes as survival needs change; the inverse is also true. Medieval society was composed of small self-sufficient communities in which serfs labored for nobles and clergy. Even though the serfs worked hard for the upper classes' benefit, the results of their labor—direct production of food and shelter—was tangible; further, the world was so limited by the manor and the church that there was little possibility of questioning the social order.

As the bourgeoisie grew and challenged the rule of the feudal aristocracy, social relations changed. By the time capitalist states came into being, the relations of production had changed drastically.[2] Workers' wage labor had developed where previously there had existed the labor of peasants, now thrown off the land. They worked for capitalists in a different system than previously existed. With no land to return to, these people were forced to work fourteen and sixteen hours a day for wages less than adequate for survival and with no guarantee that work would always be there for them. Where the serf or peasant had been guaranteed only subsistence for hard labor, the independent worker was not even sure of that. Additionally, the social relations of capitalist production created greater divisions between people and increased their alienation.[3]

In light of this history, illuminated by the class struggle involved in it, we can look clearly at aspects of culture, knowing that we will not be observing abstract universals. History is dialectical—mutual ex-

[2] It is not possible here to go into detail on the rise of capitalism. A few books which might be of use for this are Robert Latouche, *The Birth of Western Economy* (New York: Harper & Row, 1967) and Maurice Dobb, *Studies in the Development of Capitalism* (New York: International Publishers, 1964). Marx's historical works, especially *The Eighteenth Brumaire of Louis Bonaparte* (New York: International Publishers, 1963), are invaluable for understanding the functioning of people and groups within the emerging capitalist state.

[3] This will be covered in more detail in the section "Consciousness and Alienation in Marxism" (pages 19–27).

istence of opposites creates the possibilities (and necessities) of change. The negation already exists in the present reality. Capitalism itself can be best understood dialectically. It is a repressive system for the new class of workers, but it brings freedom to the bourgeoisie previously subservient to the aristocracy. This is one of the contradictions of capitalism. Another is that as capitalism creates a working class that it then exploits, the development of that class seals the fate of the capitalist system, for the working class will overthrow the bourgeois class.

The mutual existence of opposites can be found in human behavior all the time. The double-bind situation (further discussed in "Antipsychiatry," pages 101–136) represents the existence of contradictions, as do so many aspects of behavior. The realization of the unfreedom of the person placed in the double-bind is the impetus for his rebellion against those in power.

It is necessary to see Marxism as a method, not a science. While Marx's grasp of alienation and political economy can teach us how to investigate many aspects of the world, we should not rely on Marxism as codified science or dogma. The importance is the *method*. It is a method that reverses the usual mode of approaching reality; this is necessarily true, since Marxism is the method that reflects the overthrow of class society. Marxism posits the human being as an active being, one who can change her world. Taking into account class history and struggle, dialectical reality becomes clearer. For instance, it might seem difficult to understand why psychology came to the fore around the start of this century. A Marxist approach would enable one to explore the reasons: *we would begin with seeing psychology as the manifesta-*

tion, on a huge, technological basis, of capitalist economic relations; we would understand the role of psychology and psychiatry as mediating the economic-class structure and the personal-emotional structure. This mediation could then be explored to show further details; for example, personality theory in psychology presents neat packages of human development (in the psychologists' eyes), and development contrary to these suppositions becomes "abnormal." Why do the categories of normal and abnormal exist? Because psychology outlines the ethical conduct of the citizen in bourgeois society. Thus the mystery of the "science" of psychology becomes clearly the oppression by the social control functions of psychology.

Marxism's unity of theory and practice tells us why the capitalist state functions as it does: it must enforce the ideas that arise from its daily functioning. This same unity tells the masses of people that their feelings of oppression are not imaginary but reflect their true daily oppression; further, it tells us that our revolt is not simply an abnormal or isolated phenomenon but is in fact integral to our affirmation of our humanity.

History itself has changed drastically since Marx's time, but the workings of history follow the same patterns. Thus the method remains useful as long as we do not let old ideas stagnate and do not allow static models to govern us. Marxism must be rescued from the vulgar interpretations that have yielded empty rhetoric and programs based on no more than the replacement of capitalist economics with "socialist" economics. Marxism can show us that people would live their lives in totally different and liberated ways if they exercised real control; it can show us that liberation is not a goal but a way of living all the time.

The next section, "Consciousness and Alienation in Marxism," will more clearly demonstrate the relationships between economic conditions and human consciousness, and it will show that, as Jean-Paul Sartre has said, Marxism is "history itself become conscious of itself."

CONSCIOUSNESS AND ALIENATION IN MARXISM

The questions of consciousness and alienation are integral to an understanding of Marxism, as well as to Marxist psychology, where they become major questions. Recently there has been an upsurge of interest in Marx's early works, which dealt mainly with these matters. Often those people interested in "rescuing" the early Marx are simply trying to find some humanism to utilize in dissociating themselves from Marx's ideas of class struggle and proletarian revolution. This is the opposite of the "vulgar" Marxists who see an economic revolution as primary, with all other matters secondary. What is needed is an understanding of Marxism as a method of seeing all the social relations of capitalist society as a unity.

From 1841 to 1844 Marx criticized German idealist philosophy in the manner of an educated young man not yet quite sure in what direction he was going. But the basic questions began to appear, although in somewhat idealistic forms. In "A Contribution to the Critique of Hegel's Philosophy of Right," an article in the *Deutsch-Franzoische Jahrbucher,* Marx speaks of the state and society producing a "perverted world consciousness," yielding "illusory happiness," especially in relation to religion.[4] At this point, however, it is philosophy that Marx looks to for unmasking this alienation.[5]

In *The Holy Family* Marx's ideological struggle against the "young Hegelians" centers largely on the person becoming conscious of self through the real, material world. The young Hegelians, while remaining in the academic and journalistic professions, were concerned with what they perceived as "social problems." Marx took the question a step further, showing why the realm of ideas was insufficient for understanding the world:

> There is no need of any great penetration to see from the teaching of materialism on the original goodness and equal intellectual endowment of man, the omnipotence of experience, habit, and education, and the influence of environment on man. . . . If man draws all of his knowledge, sensations, etc., from the world of the senses and the experience gained in it, the empirical world must be arranged so that in it man experiences and gets used to what is really human and that he becomes aware of himself as a man.[6]

For Marx, consciousness and alienation are seen in a social context promoted by advancing capitalism:

> The members of civil society are not atoms. The specific property of the atom is that it has no properties and is therefore not connected with beings outside it by any relations determined by its own natural necessity.[7]

[4] Karl Marx, "Toward a Critique of Hegel's Philosophy of Right," in Lewis Feuer, ed., *Marx and Engels: Selected Writings on Politics and Philosophy* (New York: Doubleday, 1959), p. 262.

[5] Ibid., p. 263.

[6] Karl Marx and Friedrich Engels, *The Holy Family* (New York: International Publishers, 1967), p. 176.

[7] Ibid., p. 162.

A nonmaterialist view of the world leads to "false consciousness":

> The egoistic individual in civil society may in his non-sensuous imagination and lifeless abstraction inflate himself to the size of an atom, i.e., to an unrelated, self-sufficient, wantless, absolutely full, blessed being.[8]

The *Economic and Philosophic Manuscripts* are somewhat of a turning point for Marx. Rather than refuting the philosophers, he turns his attack on the political economists and begins to develop a materialist political economy. Although the *Manuscripts* are fragmentary, their progression is clear—Marx begins with political economy and shows how the division of labor and its corresponding class rule yield total alienation for the workers. Further, there is a dialectic interaction between political economy and alienation; this interaction continues infinitely to create new material conditions, as well as new forms of consciousness and alienation.

Marx saw the worker becoming more and more pauperized as the capitalist gained. That this pauperization has not reached its complete development is due to the strength of working-class struggles throughout the history of capitalism, but the general trend is still there (as in the current situation in the United States today). The labor power of the worker not only produces goods and services but also "produces" itself. The social relationships arising from capitalist production cause the worker to exist on subsistence wages in the nuclear family, which supposedly insures a next generation of docile workers. The worker is reified, made into an object; his human person is treated physically and ideologically as a producing object.

8 Ibid.

Since the goods produced are independent of the worker's desire to produce them, the goods are an *objectification of labor*. To explore the dimensions of this objectification, take the example of a worker in Lordstown producing Chevrolet Vegas. The worker submits to authoritarian and dangerous working conditions, often unable to talk to the worker next to him on the line; he contributes one bolt to the production of a car that he knows is dangerous on the highway and that he can only own by further putting himself in the hands of lending institutions. The more a worker produces, the more intangible it becomes, since workers are not producing for their own needs but for the needs of the boss. Alienation from the end point—the product—is one of the forms of alienation Marx points to. He also points to alienation from the process itself. Marx shows the third type of alienation, "species alienation," as a synthesis of the first two, arising from the worker becoming no more than a producing unit who is isolated from coworkers and neighbors.

As Marx put it, the worker is not "at one with his life-activity." The worker's reflection is in a world that he has created but of which he shares no part. There is no producing and sharing community but simply a maze of different work places that the worker services without taking part in the results of human work.[9]

The division of labor dialectically interacts with the alienated labor of the worker. Mental health workers, for instance, work in alienating environments in which they are supposed to help the inmates. But the hierarchy and the hospital's division of labor sets up

[9] *Economic and Philosophic Manuscripts*, in T. B. Bottomore, ed., *Karl Marx: Early Writings* (New York: McGraw-Hill, 1964), pp. 124–129.

different tasks for the different workers and professionals. The doctor is theoretically charged with therapeutic responsibility, the attendant with subordinate responsibilities that amount to little more than janitorial and custodial tasks. In reality, the doctor is a supervisor and the attendant is the only real staff member who has any human relationship with the patients; however, the hospital's needs for clear-cut responsibilities prevent furtherance of worker-patient relationships, since they would result in both groups allying against the hospital administration. Company unions, nursing supervisors, doctors, and administrators join together to play off the workers and patients against each other. The division of labor is the "economic expression of the social character of labor within alienation" as well as "the principle motive force in the production of wealth once labor is recognized as the essence of private property."[10]

In *The German Ideology,* written with Engels in 1845, Marx refutes the classical idealism of German philosophy, which saw a world of ideas rather than of tangible social relationships. In opposition to the "phantoms formed in the human brain," we are given a materialist basis of consciousness:

> Men are the producers of their conceptions, ideas, etc. —real, active men, as they are conditioned by a definite development of their productive forces and of their intercourse corresponding to these, up to the furthest forms. Consciousness can never be anything else than conscious existence, and the existence of men is their actual life process. . . . We set out from real, active men, and on the basis of their real life-processes we demonstrate the development of the ideological reflexes and echoes of this life-process.[11]

10 Ibid., p. 181.
11 Karl Marx and Friedrich Engels, *The German Ideology* (New York: International Publishers, 1969), p. 14.

The ideas of the ruling class are in every epoch the ruling ideas, i.e., the class, which is the ruling material force of society, is at the same time its ruling intellectual force.[12]

Some people who feel that alienation and consciousness were of no concern to Marx after 1845 have disregarded a major work, the *Grundrisse*. Written in 1857–1858, the *Grundrisse* is actually the notebooks and outline for *Kapital,* the *Critique of Political Economy,* and for Marx's later work in general. The concept of alienation runs throughout the *Grundrisse,* always interconnected with politics and economy and showing the fullness of Marx's understanding of the world. Money was spoken of as a symbol of alienation in capitalist society:

But just as exchange value grows, the power of money grows too; that is, the exchange relationship establishes itself as a force externally opposed to the producers, and independent of them. What was originally a means to the furtherance of production becomes a relationship alien to the producers.[13]

Marx continued the theory of species alienation, stressing that the universality of alienation derived from the universality of capitalist production.[14] We are also presented with the false view of seeing certain relationships as purely personal when they are defined by the economic conditions:

In money relationships, in the developed exchange relationships (and it is this semblance that is so seductive in the eyes of democrats), the ties of personal dependence are in fact broken, torn asunder, as also the

[12] Ibid., p. 39.
[13] Karl Marx, *The Grundrisse,* ed., and trans., David McLellan (New York: Harper & Row, 1971), p. 61.
[14] Ibid., p. 71.

differences of blood, educational differences, etc. (the personal ties all appear at least to be *personal* relationships). Thus the individuals appear to be independent (though this independence is merely a complete illusion and should rather be termed indifference); independent, that is, to collide with one another freely and to barter within the limits of this freedom. They appear so, however, only to someone who abstracts from the conditions of existence in which these individuals come into contact.[15]

When the product of our labor is taken away from us, we are supposed to find satisfaction in a maze of money relationships. The classic "keeping up with the Joneses" is an expression of the economic-status competition among alienated working people. Unable to produce what they want, they are presented with a family-, school-, and media-instilled social training that leads them to buy products that will give them friendship, sexual satisfaction, and personal salvation. What has been called consumerism is a manifestation of these alienated relationships to products that other workers have created and that provide an economic gain for the capitalist owners of production.

Marx's *Critique of Political Economy* (1859) polished up some of the preceding views. From it comes the following classic quote, which best outlines the Marxist view of consciousness formation:

In the social production which men carry on they enter into definite relations that are indispensable and independent of their will; these relations of production correspond to a definite stage of development of their material powers of production. The sum total of these relations of production constitute the economic structure of society—the real foundations, on which rise legal and political superstructures and to which cor-

15 Ibid., p. 72.

respond definite forms of social consciousness. The mode of production in material life determines the general character of the social, political, and spiritual processes of life. It is not the consciousness of men that determines their existence, but, on the contrary, their social existence determines their consciousness.[16]

Kapital too deals with aspects of alienation and consciousness, particularly "fetishism of commodities," the mystification of nature and the human relation to nature, and the transformation of human beings by their acting on and changing the external world.[17] Marx always comprehended that economic relationships could not be understood in isolation from the interpersonal relationships they created. Throughout Marx's work is the unity of all aspects of life in capitalist society. Consciousness and alienation are not separated from the daily work of the masses of people. To categorize different parts of Marxism is to lose the totality of the society that he described. In locating people's living situations in the context of their work relations and the operations of the society as a whole, Marxism offers the method for fully *knowing and acting to change* the world. Most people in the United States are working people who have spent their lives building a nation whose rulers increasingly revoke the few allowable goods and privileges. The trend today is toward the workers taking back what they have created and is theirs.

With this Marxist methodology, valuable knowledge of the world can be obtained from many sources. Mao Tse-tung applied Marxism to the particular con-

---

[16] Karl Marx, Preface to *Critique of Political Economy* in Feuer, ed., *Marx and Engels,* p. 43.

[17] Karl Marx, *Kapital,* 3 vols. (New York: International Publishers, 1969), 1: 71–72, 79–80, 130–131, 133, 177.

ditions of China, while refining the method itself. Some of his observations on human relationships are presented next. Following that, existential-phenomenological psychology is explored, with Marxism as the guide to extracting its good points. The chapter ends with some ideas on recent advances in Marxism which provide background for much of what follows.

SOME POINTS FROM MAO

Mao Tse-tung's *Four Essays on Philosophy* offer some important ways of looking at the world and of searching for some basic principles of Marxist psychology. In "On Practice" Mao is concerned with how we "know" things, a fundamental problem that differentiates Marxism from bourgeois thought, "objectivity" from "subjectivity," and even the perceptions of a mental patient from the perceptions of a psychiatrist.

For Mao, knowledge is not pure or value-free—it comes from the world view of the observer. Thus, whereas he sees two stages of cognition (phenomenal, and judgment and inference), the change from the first level to the second is based on a dialectical materialist outlook and comes about through social practice. In turn, social practice alters the reality of things, and a new reality is perceived. The dialectic is eternal, always changing: "Practice, knowledge, again practice, and again knowledge. This form repeats itself in endless cycles, and with each cycle the content of practice and knowledge rises to a higher level."[18]

Underneath this eternal change is the basic view of dialectics, the "universality of contradiction," which Marx spoke of a century earlier. In "On Contradic-

[18] Mao Tse-tung, "On Practice," *Four Essays on Philosophy* (Peking: Foreign Language Press, 1968), p. 20.

tion" Mao shows how all things contain their opposites: "The universality or absoluteness of contradiction has a two-fold meaning. One is that contradiction exists in the process of development of all things, and the other is that in the process of development of each thing a movement of opposites exists from the beginning to the end."[19] This exists on many levels. Capitalism has its roots in late feudalism and comes to power with the death of feudalism, a death in which it plays a dialectical role. But the very existence of capitalism implies the capital-labor antagonism, which breeds socialism, which will overthrow capitalism. The physics of Newton overturns earlier physics but also makes available new concepts, which will give rise to quantum theory, which will in turn transcend Newtonian physics. Our state imprisons people in jails and mental hospitals where the contradictions become heightened and people begin to fight for their freedom. The government drafts workers into the army, where they learn to use the weapons they will later use in revolutionary activities.

A thing, an event, is not pure or abstract—it only has meaning in its social context. Since the social context always changes, "the movement of change in the world of objectivity is never-ending and so is man's cognition of truth through practice."[20] When we view reality as an infinite set of contradictions, we are able to experience and understand different levels of reality. For example, a person comes to therapy because she/he feels persecuted by "forces." One level of reality is that this is strange to most people, especially to the psychiatrist. Thus the psychiatrist treats her/him on the level of strangeness without accepting

[19] Mao Tse-tung, "On Contradiction," ibid., p. 30.
[20] Ibid.

the validity of her/his feelings. Another level of reality is that this person is in fact persecuted by real people, not by abstract forces. We can understand her/his perception of forces, since we know it is socially dangerous to accuse the real persecutors. As we come to know better this person, we will find out more about her/his world and its different levels, levels that on the surface are simply contradictions centered around the same level but that really pertain to different levels. In general, we can only see the different levels of reality on which we operate by first seeing the contradictions on the surface level.

Mao's ideas on criticism and self-criticism are important in relation to problems of psychology. He sees criticism and self-criticism as the only way to resolve contradictions among the people (when there is no class struggle going on, such as that between peasants and landlords, workers and bosses). This is something our movement in the United States has widely adopted in an attempt to synthesize the political and the personal, to become more open to each other. In creating a new psychology, we are trying to create new ways of relating to each other. Hidden differences or masked feelings are a block, and only through criticism, self-criticism, can this be overcome.

In "Combat Liberalism" Mao offers additional analysis concerning the ways in which comrades are not honest with each other. Particularly, we learn the dangers of seeing personal feelings as political, and vice versa: if we don't like a person, it is dishonest to say instead we don't like his politics; if we don't like someone's political views, we should not disguise this as dislike for him as a person. Mao also speaks of the dishonesty of ignoring disagreements because they are with an old friend, of criticizing in private rather than to the face of those being criticized, of letting ideas slip by if they don't affect you personally.[21] These are matters that we encounter in all areas of life, and they are certainly applicable to psychology. A Marxist psychology ought to seek ways of relating to people honestly, and these points from Mao offer some direction for that.

Mao's ideas, particularly in *Combat Liberalism,* may seem simplistic or obvious. I would agree that they are obvious and that much of the world is obvious if we learn how to look at it—we don't discover new things as much as we discover new ways of looking at familiar things. Politics, in its essence, concerns relations among people. To this purpose Mao's philosophical writings clarify many important points.

A FEW THOUGHTS ON EXISTENTIAL-PHENOMENOLOGICAL PSYCHOLOGY

Many of us have learned much about actual relations among people, and about our own behavior, from psychologists and psychiatrists of the existential-phenomenological school. Ludwig Binswanger was the clearest of the older existentialist psychologists, and his greatest influence was on R. D. Laing and others of the antipsychiatry school.

Beginning as a counter to positivism in psychology, existentialism first drew from its philosophical sources (Søren Kierkegaard was a major influence), but it soon applied itself more to the real world of people, where it offered *the origins of a materialist psychology*. Consciously placing the human being

[21] Mao Tse-tung, "Combat Liberalism," *Five Articles* (New York: China Books).

within the framework of the surrounding world, existential psychology avoided placing existence in compartments of "objective values." It departed from the idealism of seeing human consciousness as isolated from the material world and offered a more experiential mode of understanding human behavior.

Existential-phenomenological psychology looks at the intention of human experience and behavior, seeing this intention as the constant reorganization of the situation in reference to the experience and the results of the experience. This intention is often in the realm of unfreedom, as in the alternate world created by "schizophrenics," a world that bypasses the oppression of the direct environment but that also causes intense suffering. Looking at Laing and Esterson's accounts in *Sanity, Madness and the Family*,[22] one sees young women conscious of acting in alternate modes. Others call them schizophrenics, but the young women themselves know they are living in a bad world and have taken on behavior designed to circumvent that world. One of the women described, Maya Abbot, provides a good example. From birth to age eight, when she was sent away from wartime London, Maya was "Daddy's little girl," unquestioningly responsive to her father's authority. When she returned from the countryside, she had learned new ways of living due to the exigencies of the war. She was more independent, as were many adolescents who had shared that experience. Now Maya wanted to study and do many things by herself to achieve autonomy. Her parents resisted this. They did not even allow her to express spontaneous affection toward them. Her mother felt that Maya was ill, since, "She doesn't

[22] R. D. Laing and A. Esterson, *Sanity, Madness and the Family*, 2d ed. (New York: Basic Books, 1971).

accept things any more. She's had to reason it out for herself." Maya felt, and rightly so, that her parents didn't think of her as a person but rather as an object, that her dad "often laughed off things that I told him and I couldn't see what he was laughing about."

Since she couldn't influence her family life, Maya began to feel that she could affect others in untoward ways—via prayer, telepathy, and the like. Her parents directly denied her real feelings and actions, particularly the sexual ones. She was so overwhelmed by this that she didn't know when to trust or mistrust her own perception and memory. Her suspicion of being an active agent, rather than a passive receiver, led her parents to say that she was ill and led her to seek ways in which she could influence her life. She then took on new ways of living, which were called schizophrenic by any number of professionals and by her parents. Maya knew pretty well what she was doing—in speaking of her parents' behavior, Maya said, "I used to think it a threat when I was younger, but I can act otherwise now." This different mode of being, the "otherwise" acting, was her intended response to the unbearable infringements upon her life by her parents.

This does not mean that all of Maya's actions (or all the actions of any person with severe problems) are totally intended. A certain expression, a particular sequence of behavior, are not necessarily intended; rather the whole being-in-the-world of the person is basically intended. Many—perhaps most—of the person's actions will be out of her control; they will have been built upon the survival world, the counterworld that she has set up for herself. This is an example of the limitations of intended action. Maya has learned to "act otherwise," but she certainly suffers—from her parents, hospitals, shrinks, and a whole world hostile to her alternative mode of living.

The counterworld fits in. I have seen people who were considered catatonics, people who stayed in one position for hours at a time or didn't speak or move in specific ways and time sequences acceptable to the socially defined norms. I have seen these people in institutional environments where no one was interested in talking to them, since they were catatonic, but when a humane person came along and expressed real interest in them, they would react in ways more "normal" than the aides and nurses who agreed with the doctors that they were "unreachable." Ken Kesey's *One Flew over the Cuckoo's Nest* is a good literary (but real) example. Chief Bromley was considered totally catatonic, yet he narrates an entire story in which he is a major actor.

Behavior is reactive, but also formative of new situations; thus we have a dialectical basis for a psychological theory. Medard Boss gives us a brilliant example of intended action, even in the utmost dread:

A woman of hardly 30 years dreamt, at a time when she still felt completely healthy, that she was afire in the stable. Around her, the fire, an ever larger crust of lava was forming. Half from the outside and half from the inside of her own body she could see how the fire was slowly becoming choked by this crust. Suddenly she was entirely outside the fire, and as if possessed, she beat the fire with a club to break the crust and let some air in. But the dreamer soon got tired and slowly she (the fire) became extinguished. Four days after this dream, she began to suffer from acute schizophrenia. In the details of the dream the dreamer had exactly predicted the special course of her psychosis. She became rigid at first and, in effect, encysted. Six weeks afterwards she defended herself once more against the choking of her life's fire, until finally she became completely extinguished both spiritually and mentally. Now for some years she has been like a burnt-out crater.[23]

Disregarding Boss's labeling, we see a clear example of intended action in which there is a synthesis of reaction to circumstances and self-directed activity; action redefines the situation. We don't know enough about this woman to grasp the circumstances leading to this breakdown, but we do know that she was going to take a certain amount of initiative from that point on. It is not a romantic story about how exciting "schizophrenia" can be; it is a description of one of the extreme situations in which many people find themselves due to the oppressive conditions of their lives. Feeding on the myth of personal problems being *only* personal, the suffering is internalized into a privatized world where self-action furthers the suffering.

Even at this point there is only a partial degree of self-action. We must not look at our theory and pat ourselves on the back for having *explained* human suffering. This is only a *way of looking* at the situation; it *outlines* the situation. To then act on this understanding means, in the broadest sense, to take part in building a revolutionary society where people will not be *driven* mad. In a narrower sense, there are immediate things that can be done—most particularly hospital- and community-organizing and the setting up of radical counterinstitutions that offer real alternatives to people. Such places would effect changes in people through self-action, and the direct, personal part of political change would begin to form. This is

[23] Medard Boss, *The Analysis of Dreams* (New York: Basic Books, 1958).

definitely a part of building toward a revolutionary society in which people *care* for and about each other.

As with Boss's patient, even in the giving up there is intention. Binswanger speaks of loss of self, in which the person gives up existential choice to the "other," the "false-self system." Even this, like suicide for many people, is a giving up, but with the consideration of having determined some part of the giving up within very well-defined limits of freedom. Suicide is not a "positive" answer. It can and should be prevented, but only in humane ways, and basically by alleviating the situation that leads to a person's wanting to kill her/himself. The position that people ought to have the "freedom" to kill themselves denies the reality of the *lack of freedom* in a person's life which leads to the "choice" of suicide.[24]

MARXISM AND ITS TRANSCENDENCE

Sartre, in his *Search for a Method,* examines some aspects of the relationship between existentialism and Marxism. His general framework is to see the context of all philosophy today as in the realm of *unfreedom.* He emphasizes that Marxism must expand to include more of the levels of reality with which the "vulgar Marxists" do not wish to deal. For Sartre, existentialism and its phenomenological method are subsidiary to Marxism in that they represent a passing world view that shares some basic assumptions with Marx-

[24] See Michael Glenn, "People's Psychiatry Sheet III—Suicide," in *Rough Times* anthology; and also Tony Colletti, "Suicide: A Civil Right or a Public Wrong?" and the *RT* collective's reply in *Rough Times,* vol. 3, no. 2 (November 1972).

ism but then is transcended by Marxism as Marxism synthesizes more aspects of the world. Marxism too will disappear at some future point, when capitalism has been replaced by global communism. As Sartre puts it:

> As soon as there will exist for everyone a margin of real freedom beyond the production of life, Marxism will have lived out its span; a philosophy of freedom will take its place. But we have no means, no intellectual instrument, no concrete experience which allows us to conceive of this freedom or of this philosophy.[25]

Massive changes in people's relationships in an increasingly decaying capitalism have begun to make certain transformations in our lives which, to a small extent, prefigure the future. But Sartre is essentially right—it is impossible to know very much of what this future freedom will be. *It is in the knowledge that it will exist, and that we can begin to taste the fruits of liberation, that we begin.*

Marxism is always transforming itself, since the material conditions are always in flux. Marx understood this even if he didn't know exactly what the changes would be. He knew that socialist revolution by those who produce the world's wealth was coming; he knew that it was not simply a revolution aimed at taking over the factories and seats of government. Marx's grasp of the totality of capitalist rule led him to see the rebuilding of a whole new world.

Modern capitalism's increasing infringements upon personal life have created a political mood that demands total transformation of all aspects of human life and work. This has been reflected in the socialist movement in that *the "personal-political" synthesis*

[25] Jean-Paul Sartre, *Search for a Method* (New York: Knopf, 1963), p. 34.

has become the greatest change in Marxism today.
Popular dissatisfaction with the false relationships we
live with has led to massive cultural revolt. Although
at first this appeared to be a middle-class phenomenon, it is now clearly visible as a part of the overall
working-class response to capitalism. Young workers
refuse the moral imperatives of bourgeois morality, of
social conformity, even of the nuclear family. The
important Lordstown strike exemplified the integration of personal dissatisfaction with work place dissatisfaction. Increasingly, working-class militancy
incorporates the total life experience in its confronta-
tion with sex roles, personal competitiveness, and
other conditions of daily life.

Women workers' confrontations with sexism, and
Third World workers' confrontations with racism, are
class actions that tear at the fabric of capitalist work
relations. Fighting sexism and racism leads to class
unity, since those divisions have been so instrumental
in keeping the people apart. At the same time, the
struggle builds a more human environment in which
people can learn to cooperate in creating a new world.
Wilhelm Reich understood this in part—his attempt
to integrate sexual and cultural liberation with the
political movement was a response to the same total-
ities, although he (and the times) were less ready for
that type of politics.

Today socialist and communist groups all over the
world are taking action that reflects this totality of
revolution. Rather than focusing only on wages and
distribution, the workers of the world are fighting to
build a human community. As Marx said, "They have
a world to win."

2. The Medical Model

The concept of mental illness is analogous to that of witch-craft. In the fifteenth century, men believed that some persons were witches, and that some acts were due to witchcraft. In the twentieth century, men believe that some people are insane, and that some acts are due to mental illness.

Thomas Szasz, *The Manufacture of Madness*

THE IDEOLOGY OF MENTAL ILLNESS

Today we are confronted by a major phenomenon in our society: mental illness. Moral judgments, institutional incarceration, legal codes, and popular prejudices which define mental illness are basic features of our society. Mad people are no longer figures out of literature but daily matters for us. Five hundred years ago witches were a major phenomenon, and the same social definitions existed for them. As much as the witchcraft fears of that time were strong currents in economic, political, and social life, the same is true today of mental illness. And "mental illness" is as nebulous a definition, as false a classification, and as political a label as "witchcraft" used to be.

The label of "mental illness," especially when it results in commitment to a mental hospital, is essentially a disciplinary measure against persons of the working class. When the schools, family, church, and other social institutions have not taught a person to conform, the state hospital is present to finish the task. What is called mental illness is nothing but a political classification, relative to history, class, sex, race, and many other basic factors in the social order. To demonstrate this, it is necessary to review some of the history of mental illness before turning to present-day examples of its political power as a form of social control.

As the Middle Ages came to an end, leprosy, the scourge of centuries, disappeared as a major disease. There had been nineteen thousand leprosaria in the Christian world to accommodate the huge numbers of people afflicted with the dread illness. Attached to these institutions was a set of values that made it rather easy for Western society to accept a new form of illness—illness of the mind.

As Michel Foucault puts it: "What doubtless remained longer than leprosy, and would persist when the lazar houses had been empty for years, were the values and images attached to the figure of the leper as well as the meaning of his exclusion, the social importance of that insistent and fearful figure which was not driven off without first being inscribed within a sacred circle."[1]

Foucault's thesis is that the scapegoat values derived from suffering lepers were transformed into the scapegoat values attached to the new crop of social outcasts—the mentally ill. Although this may not be the case exactly, the type of transformation seems rather well put: social values of powerful and powerless groups continue, even after the initial impetus (in

[1] Michel Foucault, *Madness and Civilization,* trans. Richard Howard (New York: Pantheon, 1965), p. 6.

this case, leprosy) disappears. The power relationships of "caring" for the lepers had created certain prerogatives for church and secular rulers, prerogatives of setting up and controlling the institutions for the lepers and of guarding the health of the general public. When new social forces brought new beliefs and new behavior, the same prerogatives could be transformed to deal with mental illness.

What were these new social forces, and how does it come to be that mental illness is a "new" feature of the beginning of capitalism? After a few centuries of sharp conflict between rising capitalists and dominant feudal rulers, the former group came to exercise sufficient power to create a capitalist Europe. Wealth accumulated by Italian merchants and bankers provided impetus to a trend set in motion since the ninth-century Viking invasions. The voyages of discovery opened up new trade routes, which enabled the capitalists to expand their power via greater wealth. A result of this was the rise of the nation-state, in Louis XIV's France.

Tied to this political development was the change in beliefs and values. A rising bourgeoisie required a work ethic and strong sense of individualism to pursue the difficult paths of capital accumulation. One aspect of this was the birth of Protestantism, which provided social and religious bases for the character structure created by capitalism. Another aspect was the individual's problems in facing a changing world—serfs were no longer tied to the land as before and had thus lost their self-contained community. In many cases displaced serfs who found no entrance into the new world of the workshop and factory wound up on the streets as beggars, prostitutes, and petty "criminals."

This social chaos fit into the framework of values

discussed above, and the result was the proliferation of houses of confinement. The Hôpital Général and other Parisian asylums contained, in the seventeenth century, one percent of the city's population, the inmates usually obtained by police roundups of beggars.[2] Foucault's position is: "Throughout Europe, confinement had the same meaning, at least if we consider its origins. It constituted one of the answers the seventeenth century gave to an economic crisis that affected the entire Western world: reduction of wages, unemployment, scarcity of coin. . . ."[3] What was happening was that the idle population, the unemployed, were being dealt with in a manner designed to make society forget about them as a problem. Frequently local government and/or capitalists made use of the inmates as a source of extraordinarily cheap labor, although at least Foucault feels it to have been unprofitable in the end.[4] Nevertheless, those in power felt that they were making economic gains at the time, much like the Southern planters in the antebellum United States.

At the same time, the new standards of morality were taught to the asylum inhabitants. To fortify this, references to madness in the Bible and the classics were dredged out. Prophets and seers, among other mad people in the Bible, were used to provide some pseudohistorical background for current treatment of those labeled mentally ill.

According to Foucault, "No medical advance, no humanitarian approach was responsible for the fact that the mad were gradually isolated, that the monotony of insanity was divided into rudimentary

2 Ibid., pp. 35, 40, 49.
3 Ibid., p. 49.
4 Ibid., p. 53.

types. It was the depths of confinement itself that generated the phenomena; it is from confinement that we must seek an account of this new awareness of madness."[5] If this is the case, and we know from present-day practices that it is, then where did the whole madness concept come from? Were there lunatics in classical times? Were prophets and sages functional lunatics, as some anthropologists would have us believe shamans are? It is wiser to see these prototypical madmen as projected types of the material conditions at the time. Rather than a new awareness of madness, the social conditions were now creating a new definition for many earlier "misfits."

The same is true for the "discovery" of witchcraft. The fourteenth and fifteenth centuries saw the development of a body of religious law concerning witches. It is certainly no accident that the Catholic Church's antiwitch campaign parallels the rise of Protestantism and heresy within the church. Those accused of witchcraft were for the most part women who had provided to other women services forbidden by lay and religious law: midwifery, medical care, abortion, counseling. To suppress these women and to keep other women in their place, witch-hunting came into being. Jacob Sprenger and Heinrich Krämer, authors of the 1494 classic on witchcraft, *Malleus Maleficarum* (Witches' Hammer) were avowedly antiwoman.

These Dominican inquisitors stated that "all witchcraft comes from carnal lust, which in women is insatiable."[6] We also know that those accused of being witches were usually poor people and that many accusations were made for personal or political rea-

---

[5] Ibid., p. 224.
[6] Quoted in Szasz, *Manufacture of Madness*, p. 80.

sons.[7] We now know that the attitude toward witches was a reflection of the feudal ruling class's attempt to destroy what was both a popular religious sentiment and a subversive social movement. Probably a majority of women accused of witchcraft were rebels who provided medical service—including abortions—to female serfs who had no access to physicians.[8] Many witches experimented with hallucinogenic drugs[9] and engaged in socially unacceptable sexual relations. The decaying feudal order began witchcraft prosecutions as part of the attempt to hold on to power. Rising capitalism accepted a good deal of the witchcraft hysteria since it fit into the antiwoman, antipopular-control attitudes that were necessary to discipline the masses in work ethic, religious and moral character, and sexual control.

While the witches were being killed, the mentally ill were being discovered and put aboard "ships of fools," whereas in earlier times they had been cared for by their local communities. This did not, however, involve large numbers of people, and they were most likely rebels against the social order or organically ill (epileptic, brain-damaged, etc.). As witchcraft died down as a "reality" in the popularized conceptions, mental illness was conceived to take its place—insane asylums sprung up during the height of witch-hunting, then took over the same social-control functions.

[7] See A. D. J. Macfarlane, *Witchcraft in Tudor and Stuart England* (New York: Harper & Row, 1970).

[8] An excellent source is Barbara Ehrenreich and Deirdre English, *Witches, Midwives, and Healers*, $1.15 from Feminist Press, Box 334, Old Westbury, N.Y. 11568.

[9] Michael J. Harner, "The Role of Hallucinogenic Plants in European Witchcraft," in Michael J. Harner, ed., *Hallucinogens and Shamanism* (New York: Oxford University Press, 1973).

Witch-hunts had more than just moral and religious grounds—they were profitable, since the witches' property was seized by the authorities and accusers often received fees. The same would come to be true of those incarcerated in mental institutions. Of course, the same power relationships carried over from witch-hunts to mad-hunts as from leprosaria to asylums. Rosen rightly states: "The bourgeois family, its property relations and moral obligations, provided the standard of rationality, and those who overstepped the limits were judged accordingly."[10] By this time the judging had been transformed to fit within a more institutional framework. The beggars and other lumpen elements in the asylums could now be called mad, since they certainly exhibited mad behavior due to their horrid living conditions in the institutions.

The transition from witch-hunts to insane asylums is sometimes difficult to understand due to the ingrained beliefs concerning illness. A good example is Szasz's description of the test by "swimming," employed to determine if a person really was a witch. The accused was completely tied up and thrown into the water; she was guilty if she floated, innocent if she sank—and three dunkings could be administered to be sure of the truth. "The aims and results of several methods of psychodiagnosis resemble closely the ordeal by water. One is the use of projective tests—like the Rorschach or the Thematic Apperception Test. When a clinical psychologist administers this test to a person referred by a psychiatrist, there is the tacit expectation that the test will show some 'pathology.' "[11]

---

[10] See George Rosen, *Madness in Society* (New York: Harper & Row, 1968), p. 169.

[11] Szasz, *Manufacture of Madness*, p. 34.

The psychological-psychiatric establishment has any number of other "tests" by which arbitrary judgments on sanity or insanity are made. Such is the case with commitment—regardless of how together a person feels, commitment will make him feel crazy, and that is all the proof needed by the authorities. Stories abound of how people are incarcerated "by accident" in mental hospitals and how their protestations against it are taken as indications of mental illness. The nature of the mind tests put over on people by the shrinks makes them impossible to escape from—just as to act angry at mental hospitalization is regarded as crazy, there is also a "symptom" in which a person acts "normal" in order to get out. It's a double-bind; you're damned if you do and damned if you don't.

The rules are so broadly defined that anyone can be considered mentally ill. Prisoners in mental hospitals have done things that everyone has done—case reports describe symptoms such as "sexual acting-out," "low self-esteem," "antiauthority attitudes," "failure to sublimate emotions." All our attitudes and behavior are open to psychiatric examination, and if we're caught in the wrong place, there is no way out.

What is the wrong place? It is any place in the society which is considered by those in power as bad; the wrong place is being the wrong class, race, or sex. Most prisoners in state psychiatric hospitals are working class, most are women, and third world people make up a disproportionate percentage of the patient population in relation to the general population. The social context of present-day America is of class, sex, and race oppression, and those oppressed by these social relations are the prime candidates for the brain police. Psychiatric commitment is a last line of defense for the ruling class against the working class.

The employment of the label of mental illness, specifically when used to jail people in asylums, is a political act. The social relations mentioned above form the core of that political action. The additional factors that become clear in daily living form the next layer—personal problems among people often lead one of them into a mental hospital, and it is easy to learn this from reading commitment proceedings. But of course, those led into commitment by parents, husbands, teachers, and others, are typically people who fit into the various categories of oppressed groups. Thus we hear of many housewives committed because they are fed up with having sole responsibility for house and children and rebel against the continuation of that role; similarly we hear of many youths, particularly female, committed by their parents for freely expressing their sexuality.

Various psychological experiments are cited from time to time in order to show the antiwoman apsects of psychology and psychiatry.[12] Clinicians' opinions of mental health and mental illness correspond to their opinions of the correct character makeup of males and females. For example, they see female sexual aggression as pathological but male sexual aggression as normal. The examples are endless. As people begin to fight back, the psychologists answer the battle cry and come up with studies of the women's movement which tell us that feminists are acting out sexual frustrations and other "pathological" conditions.

[12] Especially useful is Phyliss Chesler, *Women and Madness* (New York: Doubleday, 1972) and Naomi Weisstein's classic "Psychology Constructs the Female" (The New England Free Press). Also in Phil Brown, ed. *Radical Psychology* (New York: Harper & Row, 1973).

When social forces become threatening, the state places more and more regulations on those involved. Bourgeois society has come to such a point that more and more people are being classified as mentally ill, since we don't look for any other way to deal with them. Correspondingly, the trend in psychiatric classification has been one of "expand, expand"—if someone's behavior doesn't fit into an existing category, a new psychological category is discovered. The majority of mental hospital patients are labeled schizophrenic but even assuming they *are* mentally ill, their nearly infinite differences certainly render the catchall category of schizophrenia meaningless.

The expansion of psychiatric and psychological power has come about to satisfy the needs of bourgeois society. If smoking grass, making love, and political activity lead people into mental hospitals, obviously there are values at stake here. F. J. Braceland, testifying in 1961 as representative of the American Psychiatric Association, told the Senate Subcommittee on Constitutional Rights of the Mentally Ill: "If a man brings his daughter to me from California, because she is in manifest danger of falling into vice or in some way disgracing herself, he doesn't expect me to let her loose in my hometown for that same thing to happen."[13] Certainly the question here is one of sexual morality, not of disease. But of course the shrinks can defend this kind of imprisonment by simply "discovering" a condition of "schizophrenia with sexual acting-out" or "sociopathic behavior" or whatever else enters their minds. As guardians of morality, the psychiatric-psychological establishment

[13] Quoted in Thomas S. Szasz, *Law, Liberty, and Psychiatry* (New York: Macmillan, 1963), p. 61.

must put into the textbooks the definitions of mental illness that best reflect the dominant social values of the bourgeoisie.

In our society children grow up with highly stereotyped images of mental illness. Thomas Scheff has some interesting material on this in his *Being Mentally Ill*.[14] Comics, parents' threats of the "boogie man," and day-to-day socialization show the child that there are clear boundaries that must be observed. Scheff also traces the mental illness imagery to adulthood. He quotes studies on the portrait of mental illness in the mass media. In the same way that blacks are mentioned in newspapers (e.g., "Black Man Robs Store"), former mental patients are dealt with:

> Because of highly biased reporting, the reader is free to make the unwarranted inference that murder and rape and other acts of violence occur more frequently among former mental patients than among the population at large. Actually it has been demonstrated that the incidence of crimes of violence (or any crime) is much lower among former mental patients than in the general population.[15]

If one observes people's daily conversation, numerous references to stereotyping of mental illness jump out. It seems that this stereotype is an integral part of the socialization process and probably increases as the number of persons labeled mentally ill grows. The contradictions have been heightened in recent years, and the popular attitudes are under growing attack.

EXPOSING THE MYTH

How can the criticism by Szasz and others of the medical model be "proved"? Probably the best ex-

[14] Thomas J. Scheff, *Being Mentally Ill: A Sociological Theory* (Chicago: Aldine, 1971), pp. 64–76.
[15] Ibid., p. 72.

ample to date is the experiment conducted by David Rosenhan and his colleagues.[16] Eight people, posing as persons worried about their mental health, were admitted to various mental hospitals on the East and West coasts solely on the basis of reporting having heard voices. They were truthful about their real life history and extremely cooperative with hospital staff. As soon as they were admitted, they said the voices had stopped and they felt fine. Still, all but one were classified as schizophrenic (the other was labeled a manic-depressive), and they were held for periods of up to fifty-two days. When released, none was considered "cured" but rather "under remission." During the whole time, no staff member discovered that any of the eight was an imposter, although some patients were aware of it.[17] When psychiatrists at one of the hospitals were informed of the experiment, they expressed disbelief. Rosenhan told them to watch for more "pseudopatients." Sure enough, the shrinks "detected" forty-one people posing as insane and found twenty-three others judged sane by at least one psychiatrist. Rosenhan then informed the psychiatrists that *none of these people were pseudopatients*, that he had not sent in any more phonies!

Many other experiments have proven the invalidity of psychiatric classification. If two groups of psychology students are given identical sets of data from patient evaluations, they will find mental illness if told

[16] Jackie Christeve, "The Rosenhan Experiment: Psychiatric Myths Exposed," *Rough Times,* vol. 3, no. 4 (February–March 1973), p. 8.

[17] Real patients were aware, since the pseudopatients did not behave as if they had been accustomed to the label of mental illness and had never learned the mental patient role. Staff members were unaware, since they are not part of the inmate society (patients learn to speak differently with staff than with patients).

beforehand that the data are from patients; if they are told the data are from upstanding members of the community, no pathology will be determined. Scheff reports studies of commitment hearings which show that psychiatrists take an average of five minutes to determine mental illness in people whom they have never seen before.[18]

The nonsense of psychiatric classification only makes sense when it is seen as a bluff. In the interests of enforcing social discipline on patients, psychiatry and psychology make judgments based on the class perspective their practitioners have been taught. Even when unaware of what they are doing, psychiatrists and clinical psychologists inevitably diagnose working-class people as insane, since working-class people do not exhibit the textbook stereotypes of middle-class behavior. Such a system feeds on itself, transmitting diagnostic criteria through all levels of training. Further, through popularized articles and television shows, the public is taught to believe in these same criteria.

Psychiatric "reality" next crosses into the mental institution itself, creating a social structure that is a lower rung of the society as a whole.

THE SOCIAL STRUCTURE OF THE
MENTAL HOSPITAL

The social structure of the mental hospital (particularly the state hospital) is, at the same time as it is a microcosm of the society outside, functioning as a disciplinary arm of the bourgeois state. Essentially it is based on a scarcity economy. In addition to the scarcity of money and material goods, the mental

18 Scheff, *Being Mentally Ill*, p. 133.

hospital deals in terms of the scarcity of emotional support, civil rights, physical place/privacy, etc. It is a *total institution,* as described so brilliantly in Erving Goffman's *Asylums,* having control over all aspects of a person's life—waking, sleeping, eating, work.

Mental hospitals reinforce (re-enforce) the culture and morality of bourgeois America. Hard work, faith in one's superiors, and rule-following are taught, backed up with the wide range of threats available to the hospital staff. Everything done *to* the patients is seen as something *for* the patients—"work therapy," "recreational therapy," etc. Thus cheap labor on the wards and in "occupational therapy" is obtained in the guise of help. The worker, oppressed by wage slavery on the outside, is retrained for it inside the hospital. Mass use of drugs like Thorazine decrease the energy level of patients, making them as malleable as the administration desires. They then must perform their role functions: "playing" patient, doing work, etc. The alternatives are a wide range of punishments like electroshock and isolation, which are also masked as "therapeutic."

A pecking order is set up in the hospital to create a microsociety. Doctors are on top, psychologists below doctors, nurses below them, aides below nurses, and patients on the bottom. Nurses and aides have others controlling them, and they are encouraged to control the next-lower rung. No one is allowed to question his role. Oppression comes down vertically, with all playing victim and oppressor. Patients are played off against one another, especially in the "therapeutic community" model that has been created to cover up the true nature of the hospital. Patients are encouraged to rat on others and to accept special privileges, since that is often the only way for them to survive.

The structure in medical hospitals is similar as well. The medical administrators and their boards of directors know that such hierarchies will prevent rebellion. Contrasted to this is the Chinese hospital system, in which professionals take part in janitorial work and janitorial workers aid in the care of the patients. Conferences on procedure for medical care involve relatives, coworkers, and all levels of hospital staff. Cooperation replaces competition, with the health of the patients having priority (as opposed to American hospitals, where profit, expediency, and experimentation are primary). It is not hospital care per se that has an absolute structure of hierarchy; rather, it is the social system in which the care takes place.

The absurd state of the outside world—electric Saran Wrap dispensers advertised as freeing women from the drudgeries of housework, deodorants to privatize people from each other, and so on—is used in the mental hospital. False and hollow lies propagate the powerless position of the mental patient in the most degrading manner. Take, for instance, the carnival, a popular cultural event in mental hospitals. The staff sets up a series of booths with games so simple as to make the patient a rat in a Skinner box. One such game consists of throwing a beanbag into a large ring—in fact, there are so many large rings so close to each other that it is nearly impossible to miss. If the beanbag falls in the small space outside the rings, another chance is eagerly offered. Although it may be hard to lose the games, competition is still urged. No one really loses, however, since everyone who plays is told he did well and is given a prize, like one cigarette. One can accumulate many cigarettes in this manner, and since cigarettes are a scarce item in the hospital economy, resourceful patients can get a good supply. The accumulation of cigarettes, though, is dependent on the patient's accepting many humiliating and condescending gestures from the staff, so the patient's resourcefulness is automatically turned into submission. Of course, attempts at creating a real carnival atmosphere are not allowed. Patients must follow the prescribed games and not invent any of their own.

Prohibitions against creating one's own plesaure are prevalent throughout the hospital routine. Eating is not allowed to be a pleasurable communal activity; sexual contact of any sort is not only illegal but a sign of further mental illness. This is in fact true of all activity in the hospital—any "illegal" actions of patients are seen as illness, since "normality" requires submission to the social order. Manners, attire, acceptance of authority are dictated, and release from the hospital is dependent on the *medical authorities' view of proper social conduct*. Thus a woman should return to, or search for, a family and play housewife; a youth should go home and obey his parents; a personal preference for a particular job is overruled by the demands of the staff to take one of a narrow range of nonskilled jobs regardless of the person's ability. All this affirms the lowliness of the patients' position as one who cannot choose her own life—after all, if she knew how to live correctly, she wouldn't be in the hospital in the first place.

Most of these examples of hospital life come from state hospitals, the repositories of working-class people. Private psychiatric hospitals tend to be more "caring," although that is relative to what is meant by "care." For instance, certain private institutions specialize in heavy regimens of electroshock. Middle- and upper-class patients are sent to these hospitals, usually by parents or husbands, to be trained in proper social conduct. Some of these hospitals are quite comfortable, country club–like places where psychiatrists have time to spend with patients. This is in contrast with the state hospital, where psychiatrists are the kings and administrators who zip through the wards in record time, little thought being given to the perpetuation of the myth of doctor's care.

Besides the various euphemisms that the psychiatric hospital uses for political labels and political suppression, it is important to realize that what might even pass for therapy is barely obtainable in the state hospital. The mental hospital is mainly custodial, placing most of its energy on moralizing rather than helping. Emphasis on helping people work out their problems is, in fact, frowned on. One of many examples I could give is the case of a black woman working as a psychiatric aide in a large Northeastern state hospital. She heard about a seminar on drug addiction at a nearby college which cost about thirty dollars for a weekend of several sessions. Being involved in working with addicts and ex-addicts in the ward, she asked to go, even offering to pay for it herself. The doctors felt that she didn't have enough background to get anything out of the seminar, telling her that only people of nurse rank or above could go. They were obviously afraid that she would see through the lack of caring and helping, afraid that she as an aide would try to help patients.

The professionalist structure also mirrors the basic capitalist method of categorizing people by their work and creating a division of labor that prevents unified struggle. Each member of the hospital staff has a specific function and cannot do more than is allowed. Aides and attendants are recruited from the working class to perform the majority of custodial functions (by this I mean maintenance of the patients). They are told that the patients are crazy and that they should be on guard at all times. This places them in the role of police agent for the hospital and prevents them from seeing that the people in the hospital could be their family or friends. Aides are taught that they have no role in the "therapeutic" process, and for the most part they accept this. In recent years more and more young people have been working as psychiatric aides, and some of them bring to the hospital a certain caring, an understanding that the mental hospital is not a healthy place. These young aides may attempt to engage in real communication with the patients, often entering into friendships with them. This is considered bad (i.e., dangerous to the hospital's class stratification) by the administrators, since it deprives the doctors and nurses of their unquestioned control. It is the same division of labor found in factories, large offices, department stores, etc., where people are kept from each other on the basis of job rank. Not only do the various staff persons suffer (in the sense that they are kept from uniting against the administration and doctors), but the patients bear the largest brunt of this conflict.

Like other institutions of our society, the mental hospital functions to divide people and prevent them from identifying and fighting back against their oppressors. It is imperative to view the hospital in this way, not as a benevolent or neutral place where some things go wrong by accident or on account of certain people being bad. We need new approaches to fighting the mental institutions. The beginnings of this will be dealt with later in the last chapter, "Dare to Struggle, Dare to Win!" (pages 160–169).

3. The Freud Problem

Freudianism is a major intellectual current and actual practice of United States society today. More than simply another school of psychology, psychoanalysis plays a special role in social control which transcends even its major disciples. Freud was the father of modern psychology, even if he was not the first psychiatrist. With his insight into the needs of bourgeois society, Freud represented the bourgeois response to ongoing social conditions. His view of people, history, anthropology, sexuality, and social change mirrored the realities of his time. Freud's role was, however, not to liberate but to aid in the creation of a world view that fit the needs of growing capitalism. This chapter will place that world view in its proper context, rather than simply providing an academic refutation of Freudianism.[1]

[1] Andrew Salter, *The Case against Psychoanalysis* (New York: Harper & Row, 1972), provides a decent, though not radical, critique of Freudian ideas.

The new century was an intense change from the past. Imperialist rivalry between Western nations was about to burst into open warfare. Capitalism was clearly rising to prominence, and working-class movements attacked it relentlessly. The increasingly scientific nature of capitalism required scientific explanations of human behavior; it also needed an overall explanation of how human behavior could be channeled into modes that were required by the new social order.

Freud saw an "economic" setup of human behavior. He balanced ego, id, and superego; conscious, unconscious, and preconscious; sexuality, the family, and the state. This balancing mirrored the balances of the capitalist state. Like Newtonian physics, the conservation of psychic energy was an explanation of reality based on early capitalist accumulation. The Protestant ethic, as a behavioral translation of such accumulation, was to be expanded by Freud to the point of prescribing an order of human existence that would create docile, subservient people.

Logically, the id, ego, and superego would be reified by Freud into the bases of his metapsychology. The id represented the basic activities of human beings which so frightened the ruling classes, the superego represented the social restrictions against the id, and the ego maintained the proper balance for the reality principle. Providing industrial discipline for the working class and moral training for the middle class, psychoanalysis re-created bourgeois social relations in the human and personal realm.

Unconscious, preconscious, and conscious divisions of the psyche asserted the imperfect nature of people and the blind forces that they might someday control. The unconscious served to justify the passive obedience of people to the state and to the daily operating mechanisms of the social order. Keith Brooks[2] has shown how the concept of the unconscious implies (1) the separation of subject (person) from object (material world), (2) the passive position of people in regard to "irrational" forces, and (3) the notion that people can never be in control of their own lives. Brooks points out that the practical implication of the psychoanalytic theory of the unconscious is authoritarian social control by the ruling class.

Instincts play an important role in the psychoanalytic model. As the "seething cauldron" of the id, instincts threaten the stability of society. Freud's Eros, which in a liberated view might be loving human warmth, is seen as a detriment to society which must therefore be sublimated. The sexuality of Eros had to be channeled, and Freud's codification of male supremacy served this purpose well. The Victorian period has been found to have been quite different from the textbook descriptions of a frightened, sexually up-tight society. In fact, there was a strong undercurrent of open sexuality among the working class which scared the bourgeoisie and the remaining gentry. As Kate Millett explains, the function of controlling sexuality was a main feature of Freudianism.[3]

The psychoanalytic theory of sexual sublimation posited that only through this channeling of human sexuality could patriarchal, capitalist society function. When translated into popularized moral training for

[2] Keith Brooks, "Freudianism Is Not a Basis for Marxist Psychology," in Phil Brown, ed., *Radical Psychology* (New York: Harper & Row, 1973).
[3] Kate Millett, *Sexual Politics* (New York: Doubleday, 1970).

petit bourgeois women, it was quite frightening. As a move toward the professionalization of the role of housewife, popularized Freudianism scared women into enforcing the "natural" biological development of the child. Writing about this, Florence Rush says:

> I became ripe for motherhood also at a time when urban and suburban America was finding itself fast in the grip of Freudian influence. With the beginning of popular recognition of infant sexuality and sensitivity and impressionability of infants, there grew an enormous awareness and awesome responsibility of parenthood. I was deeply impressed with the power which rested in the hands of those who cared for and raised children: the power to create an either warped or wholesome personality.[4]

Fear of the Oedipus complex ranged widely through middle-class culture. In fact, the relationship that Freud explains by Oedipal conflict is caused by the nuclear family. Psychoanalysis is simply trying to justify the universality of the Oedipus complex by asserting that this conflict requires stern parental control of the child and harsh male control of the woman. In present times the application of this is exemplified by Bruno Bettelheim's insistence that student rebellion is an acting out of Oedipal conflict. Indeed, student rebels are turning against their fathers, but for good reason—they are revolting against the patriarchy which has rendered life meaningless for them.

Generally, Freud uncovered certain realities of how people act in capitalist society. What he did with these realities, however, was to mystify them, to psychologize them into a system that told people that they

[4] Florence Rush "Who's Afraid of Margaret Ribble?" *Rough Times,* vol. 3, no. 1 (September 1972), pp. 6–8.

could never alter their world. With this understanding of the role of psychoanalysis, the remainder of this chapter will concentrate on the codified male supremacy of Freudianism, Freudian anthropology, and the failure of attempts of synthesizing Marx and Freud.

MALE SUPREMACY IN FREUDIANISM

Freud's mystified biology formed the basis for his theory of male supremacy. The authoritarian father of the "primal horde" who keeps all the women for himself and is eventually killed by his sons is the basic father in Freud's view. The tragedy of this primal experience leads to the development of civilization to protect the family and state from further patricide. With this as his historical background, Freud launches a full-scale attack on women, whom he holds responsible for the tragedy.

Psychoanalysis's antiwoman attitudes started at an earlier time, however, when Freud and Breuer published *Studies on Hysteria* in 1885.[5] The book is full of studies of women who were clearly victims of sexually repressed family life. Freud holds the women themselves responsible, basing their "conversion" symptoms (what are commonly called psychosomatic symptoms) on sexual fears rooted in childhood trauma. Though Freud saw the reality of the problem, he blamed women for it and demanded they adjust to it. Essentially, the petit bourgeois and bourgeois woman was to be passive and obedient to her husband.

The active and passive human traits of men and

[5] Sigmund Freud and Josef Breuer, *Studies on Hysteria*, trans. James Strachey (New York: Basic Books, 1957).

women were theorized more fully in *The Interpretation of Dreams*,[6] in which Freud characterized the feminine personality as passive, male-seeking, baby-suckling. Dream symbolism contained the feminine role in the unconscious: "All elongated objects, sticks, tree trunks, umbrellas, all sharp and elongated weapons, knives, daggers, and spikes represent the male member. . . . Small boxes, chests, cupboards, and ovens correspond to the female organ; also cavities, ships, and all kinds of vessels."[7]

This was all to prove female passivity and desire for penis-vagina sexuality (which Freud considered the only acceptable mode of sexual behavior). Since Freud saw dreams as wish-fulfillment, he interpreted women's dreams as nearly always seeking male penetration or other male aggressive sexuality. Interpreting a woman's dream of putting a candle into a holder, the candle breaking as she does this, Freud speaks of the candle as "an object which excites the female genitals" and the breaking of it as representing the woman's frigidity due to masturbation. Similar is the view that a woman dreaming of a man masturbating is a vicarious act of his penetration of her.[8] Women's dream symbolism, for Freud, was always to be interpreted in a negative way: "When a person of the female sex dreams of falling, this almost always has a sexual significance; she becomes a fallen woman." Also, due to female weakness, a woman's dream of carrying a man is an infantile fantasy because that is an inappropriate role reversal.[9]

[6] Sigmund Freud, *The Interpretation of Dreams,* in *Basic Writings of Sigmund Freud,* ed. and trans. A. Brill (New York: Random House, 1938).

[7] Ibid., p. 371.

[8] Ibid., pp. 253–254, 388.

[9] Ibid., pp. 264, 327.

The Oedipus complex is first mentioned substantially in *Interpretation of Dreams,* but is more fully developed five years later. Integral to this is the myth of penis envy—Freud's fantasy was that little girls, upon finding that boys have penises, feel themselves castrated and blame the mother for this. Further, the major part of the female psyche is determined by this penis loss and subsequent penis envy.[10] The female will continue to search all her life for a surrogate penis: "The desire after all to obtain the penis for which she so much longs may even contribute to the motives that impel a grown-up woman to come to analysis; and what she quite reasonably expects to get from analysis, such as the capacity to pursue an intellectual career, can often be recognized as a sublimated modification of this repressed wish."[11]

The discovery of her castration and subsequent penis envy becomes Freud's way of explaining the female tendency to perform "erroneous acts," seduction fantasies, and narcissistic, masochistic acts. As Freud saw it, narcissism arises from women having a stronger need to be loved than to love and masochism from the "constitutional" weakness in the feminine psyche.[12]

After puberty, Freud offers three choices for further development: "One leads to sexual inhibition or neurosis, the second to a modification of character in the

[10] Ibid., pp. 306–309, 377–378.

[11] Sigmund Freud, *New Introductory Lectures on Psychoanalysis,* ed. and trans. James Strachey (New York: Norton, 1965), p. 171.

[12] Sigmund Freud, *The Psychopathology of Everyday Life,* in Brill, ed., *Basic Writings,* p. 122; *New Introductory Lectures,* pp. 158, 164, 180.

sense of masculinity complex, and the third to formal feminity.[13] This first alternative is sketched out in *Studies on Hysteria*. The second, "masculinity complex," is a major point—it involves "clinging" to clitoral activity through masturbation and retaining of clitoral sensitivity; Freud sees the clitoris as unsuitable for sexual pleasure, being a "stunted penis."[14] Women must transfer sexuality to the vagina to be normal and mature: "In the transformation to womanhood very much depends upon the early and complete relegation of this sensitivity from the clitoris over to the vaginal orifice. In those women who are sexually anesthetic, as it is called, the clitoris has stubbornly retained this sensitivity."[15]

This Freudian biologism is aimed at making the woman the property of the man by asserting his control over sexual intercourse; if the clitoris were considered the organ of female sexual pleasure, then the woman could be in control of her orgasms. The "bad" things that Freud sees arising from continued clitoral pleasure are homosexuality and the furthering of "polymorphous perversity."[16] Thus natural sexual behavior is doubly prohibited—both in itself and as a failure to develop normally.

What has begun with biology has been transformed into a social ethic. We would not argue that the male sperm cell is mobile and that the female egg cell is less so. But for Freud this becomes the rationale for all

[13] Freud, *New Introductory Lectures*, p. 172.

[14] Ibid., pp. 93, 172, 177.

[15] Sigmund Freud, *A General Introduction to Psychoanalysis*, trans. J. Riviere (New York: Permabook, 1953), p. 327.

[16] Freud, *Three Contributions to the Theory of Sex*, in Brill, ed., *Basic Writings*, p. 592.

human behavior.[17] Freud, like those who hold the anticontraception and antiabortion attitudes found in today's society, is attempting to deny the woman any responsibility for her body, to deliver it up to the psychiatrists, doctors, and clergy. Of course, women's attempts to assert control will be further silenced by the "scientific reliability" of psychoanalytic theory. The number of women committed to asylums for sins against male power trips of reproduction testifies to the power of the shrinks, particularly when armed with psychoanalytic authority.

Freud's original Oedipus situation seals the fate of womankind by accusing women of inciting men to sex because of the female's "peculiar helplessness." This restatement of traditional religious dogma holds women responsible for rape. In the Middle Ages there was a legal basis for woman's responsibility when she was raped; today police, courts, and mental health professionals still echo that claim.

Women's helplessness also fits into social sublimation through the family:

> One may suppose that the founding of families was connected with the fact that a moment came when the need for genital satisfaction no longer made its appearance like a guest who drops in suddenly, and, after his departure, is heard of no more for a long time, but instead took up its quarters as a permanent lodger. When this happened, the male acquired a motive for keeping the female, or speaking more generally, his sexual object, near him; while the female who did not want to be separated from her helpless young, was obliged in her interests to remain with the stronger male.[18]

[17] Freud, *New Introductory Lectures,* p. 156.
[18] Sigmund Freud, *Civilization and Its Discontents,* trans. James Strachey (New York: Norton, 1961), p. 46.

So Freud grasps part of the development of the patriarchal family, although he justifies it in the interests of
civilization. Such a presentation claims that the institutions of society develop independently of the overall
workings of that society; it further claims that there is
no other way and therefore no possibility of change.

From this develops the notion of total female subservience. Child-rearing and man-caring are the only
real parts of a woman's life and thus should fulfill all
of her psychological and social needs. But to insure
this an official enslavement of women is required:
"Women increasingly represent the interests of the
family and of the sexual life. The work of civilization
has become increasingly the business of men; it con-
fronts them with ever more difficult tasks and compels
them to carry out instinctual sublimation of which
women are little capable."[19]

This codified division of labor between men and
women creates differences in how men and women
view their world. The middle-class woman, supposedly content with house and children, is isolated
from other people. The emotional strength that she is
required to provide for the family has no place to
develop outside that family. Freud takes this further
in his assumptions about women's attempts at com-
pensation. From the depths of his imagination, Freud
scrounges up the theory that women invented weaving
to replicate their pubic hair, the purpose of which is to
hide their "inferior" genitalia.[20] As Freud creates his
vision of female inferiority, he adds a double bind:
"The woman finds herself forced into the background
by the claims of civilization and she adopts a hostile

[19] Ibid., p. 50.
[20] Freud, *New Introductory Lectures,* p. 181.

attitude toward it."[21] Accordingly, Freud declaims women for lack of justice and social interest, as well as for their general insincerity.

The next step is to accuse the women who fail in this game of being mentally ill. Their problems are their fault, and the analyst can cure them. Women who do not conform to the passive, home-oriented life are thus enemies of civilization and need to be reeducated or put away. This is, of course, true—if women en masse refused to carry out their daily duties, what would keep everything running?

Capitalism's economic and social bases of male supremacy have been thoroughly internalized into psychoanalytic theory and practice. This operates on more levels than simply that of private psychoanalysis. Freudianism is stronger in the United States than in any other country and is the basis for an incredibly large number of training programs in such areas as clinical psychology, social work, personality theory, child psychology, sociology, anthropology, and sex education. Popularized Freudianism can be found in many newspapers and magazines; it seeps into teaching guides for public school teachers, into criminology, advertising, popular music, and many other places. Many Freudian terms are part of people's everyday language.

This pervasiveness of Freudian doctrine has been a major repressive aspect of American psychology and psychiatry. In every area of society women are held to be inferior to men, and psychoanalytic theory and practice have greatly aided the belief in that inferiority. Other aspects of the Freudian world view create

21 Freud, *Civilization*, p. 50.

an equally pessimistic picture for humans in general (except for those in high positions). This is found in the Freudian anthropology.

THE FREUDIAN ANTHROPOLOGY

Totem and Taboo, Group Psychology and the Analysis of the Ego, and *The Future of an Illusion* began the trend toward a more generalized world view in psychoanalysis. Freud was to make the definitive statement in *Civilization and Its Discontents* (1930). Reich, at the time second in importance to Freud in the Technical Seminar, opposed the ideas that Freud began to throw around. This was the major point of disagreement between Reich and Freud, the point on which there was no compromise.

In the last years before fascism took over in Germany, Freud was writing a book that spoke to the same question as did Nazi philosophies of society. A society of people whose life is totally suppressed can have different forms: Nazism brought out a monstrous, military, genocidal form; Freudianism brought out an internalized, also military, self-destructive form. Both are products of modern capitalism in which we see how the economic base of society yields certain superstructural formations that seek to prevent human freedom.

Freud's reality principle demanded that the pleasure principle be given up, since humans were incapable of "governing" themselves in terms of needs, desires, instincts. The concept of "instinct" is, of course, problematic. It is the point at which one adheres to or departs from the Freudian social theory. An honest Marxism cannot coexist with the Freudian theory of instincts. To do so is to place arbitrary categories of human personality before the fact of history, to bypass history. It means the creation of artificial categories of human consciousness directly opposed to the Marxist theory of consciousness, and these artificial categories are such as to place social change in the "impossible" category, since instincts are "primary."

There is a hidden dimension, however. Freud did not pull instinct theory out of the air. It had existed for centuries, though mainly in religions (and most religion is ultimately based on instinctual fallibility of humans). Freud simply rationalized instinct theory to place it in the new religion: psychology. That he did so shows that bourgeois society needed a new view of the family within society and a way to use it for social control. When the priests and psychoanalysts speak of instincts, they have something of a real meaning: instincts are essentially all those aspects of human freedom and spontaneity that must be crushed. This does not legitimize the concept of any particular instincts spoken of by Freud; rather it rearranges their context. In other words, the instinct called Eros is the human attempt at freedom and spontaneity; the instinct called Thanatos is the human inversion of the possibilities of freedom, taking root as aggression toward others instead of toward rulers.

Freud was most concerned with stemming Eros. Like all instincts, it had to be *sublimated* into acceptable channels. Further, Freud defined mental illness and social problems in terms of the person's ability to sublimate. For instance, in speaking of the importance of work, in a psychological restatement of the Protestant work ethic, Freud says that people "do not strive after it as they do after other possibilities of satisfaction. The great majority of people only work under the stress of necessity, and this natural human aversion to work raises most difficult social problems.[22]

Freud clearly places himself in the role of enforcer of society's status quo; he sees a world of people who are "ill" because they dislike work. In actuality, it is "healthy" to be averse to the work relations of capitalism, since most work is alienating. It is not, as the psychoanalytic model tells us, "healthy" to work for the "necessity" of capitalist society. An ordered society, as Freud envisioned it, could not tolerate the questioning of what is "given." The Freudian society accepts capitalism and channels human potential into those appropriate areas:

> The benefits of order are incontestable. It enables men to use space and time to the best advantage, while conserving their psychical forces. We should have a right to expect that order would have taken its place in human activities from the start and without difficulty; and we may well wonder that this has not happened—that, on the contrary, human beings exhibit an inborn tendency to carelessness, irregularity and unreliability in their work, and that a laborious training is needed before they learn to follow the example of their celestial models.[23]

Workers do not enjoy the alienating relationships into which they are forced. Therefore they rebel against them in various ways. They certainly do not adhere to the bourgeoisie's model of celestial regularity. Freud's attempt to theorize about the natural goodness of work was an attempt to create an overall discipline for the working class. He made no bones about saying what the needs of society were, although he did not always identify the society as a capitalist one.

Prior to Freud and the other scientific intellectuals

22 Ibid., p. 27n.
23 Ibid., p. 40.

who expounded the natural order of capitalism, religion provided theoretical and moral bases for it. Calvinism, the first ideological exposition of capitalism, posed the threat of a wrathful god who created human beings for his own purposes. In gratitude for that creation, we are to be totally subservient and accept the order given by God or, in the modern sense, by society's rulers. The prohibitions are the same too, as are their rationales: "A cultural community is perfectly justified, psychologically, in starting by proscribing manifestations of the sexual life of children, for there would be no prospect of curbing the sexual lusts of adults if the ground had not been prepared for it in childhood."[24]

If there is no doubt that Freud is a social control agent of capitalist society, let us look to his writing on the basis of capitalism—i.e., private property: "In abolishing private property, we deprive the human love of aggression of one of its instruments, certainly a strong one, though certainly not the strongest."[25] Freud assumes private property as natural and bases his theory of human aggression on that. It is a clear case of how Freud, the bourgeoisie's ideologist, built his theories on the bourgeoisie's actual society. Instead of explaining private property, Freud explains human behavior as based on private property. He leaves out the history of human and social development, since he could not explain it all away with his psychologisms. Nothing can be changed, since it is all there *before history*. Yet people still try to change things. How to stop them? Freud's military model of human personality and society led him to believe that civilization must weaken a human being's aggressive

24 Ibid., p. 51.
25 Ibid., p. 60.

instincts by "setting up an agency within him to watch over it, like a garrison in a conquered city."[26]

Some laugh at the absurdity of the orthodox Freudian theory. I would caution against laughing—Freudian theory itself is not a bullet that will kill us, but it is a manifestation of the repressive forces of the social order within which we live. Any radical person would be mistaken in ignoring the close approximation between Freudianism and the pacification techniques used in Vietnam and Attica. All those things we know as oppressive have been placed in a neat theory that reflects the way those oppressive things affect us. Gandhi was once asked what he thought of Western civilization. He replied, "It would be a good idea." What does it mean to accept, without question, the validity of the civilization which we know? Does constant war and suffering, sanctified by government, capital, and God, mean so little that we can accept it being written off as instinctual?

"Cathected libido" and unbridled "aggression" are certainly not the categories that describe liberation; they are the categories invented to mystify oppression and prevent liberation. The whole body of Freudian theory, while pointing to a certain social reality, functions as a mask that hides the facts of the world.

Given this function of Freudianism, it is incredible that many socialists have attempted to fuse Marx and Freud. The next section focuses on some of these attempts and demonstrate their impossibility.

THE FAILURE OF THE MARX-FREUD SYNTHESIS

Erich Fromm's *Escape from Freedom,* Herbert Marcuse's *Eros and Civilization,* and Reimut Reiche's

[26] Ibid., p. 69.

Sexuality and Class Consciousness are among the books that have attempted to synthesize Marx and Freud. Wilhelm Reich fits into a different category and is discussed later.

There is no possibility of a Marx-Freud synthesis. The thought of these two men is totally different, they are at odds with each other, they represent different classes and different world views.

The material on Freud in the preceding sections should make it clear that psychoanalytic social theory is a reactionary one. At every point there is a huge difference between the social control of Freud and the social revolution of Marx. Marxism sees the praxis of human beings, their active part in changing the world for themselves. People are not innately passive, nor do they function as a mass of unbridled instincts. They are participants in history because they are history. Their present history is of oppression of the many workers by the few capitalists and that was the situation even as Freud wrote in the early decades of the twentieth century. Marx saw the world differently because he was viewing it through its complete history and because he was speaking of human liberation. For Freud, there was no history; if, in fact, a chain of events occurred, it could be explained by psychoanalytic theory. Thus World War I and Leonardo da Vinci fall under the category of Freudian historical explanation—lives and events are explained away by psychologisms, the use of psychological jargon to mystify the real nature of things. For Marx, history is the total progression of human existence and experience. It *contains* everything. Marx's historical method placed, for the first time, a perspective on what appeared to be irrational forces.

Why have socialists made efforts to merge Marx

and Freud? One obvious reason is that there has been hardly any tradition of applying Marxism to personal liberation. Reich remains the foremost person to try to integrate personal and political liberation, and it is only recently that he has been so widely read. Another reason is that the material conditions have not been favorable: there was no context of a general movement involving total liberation. Workers' movements were always under attack by the bourgeoisie, and it was enough for them to survive the repression. Socialist intellectuals were typically so removed from ongoing struggle that they could not understand the daily lives of most people. Additionally, professional privilege has been a barrier to many, especially persons practicing private psychoanalysis. For such people, the revolutionary implications of Marxism would threaten their privileged position.

Erich Fromm and Herbert Marcuse come out of the so-called Frankfurt School, a group of scholars including Theodor Adorno, Georg Lukacs, and Max Horkheimer. This school was essentially social-democratic in nature, and few of its members had a clear vision of class struggle. In fact, most of them tended to obscure class differences, concentrating on pure "critical theory." Fromm and Marcuse are basically pessimistic about the possibilities of human liberation. While severely disagreeing with each other on many issues, they share common ground. The most important is their excessive reliance on Freudianism as an explanation of human behavior.

Fromm, in *Escape from Freedom,* posited a human nature with certain "fixed and unchangeable" factors. Tracing the history of totalitarian movements, Fromm saw their mass following as proof of some sort of innate submission to authority. Unlike Reich, Fromm didn't present a class analysis of that submission, nor did he offer a strategy to combat it. Relying on instincts, he retreated into a rather conservative Freudian view of human interaction. Instead of starting with the society, Fromm often started with the individual: "Any group consists of individuals and nothing but individuals, and psychological mechanisms which we find operating in a group can therefore only be mechanisms that operate in individuals."[27]

From this point Fromm went on to postulate subservience to totalitarian leaders as "principle social avenues of escape." He did not see that the authoritarian family had re-created the authoritarian state within the individual's psyche. Fromm has nothing to offer in the way of freedom—he spent much energy defending United States "democracy" and disregarded socialist revolution as an alternative.

In his writings on Marxism, Fromm focused on the "humanism" of the "early Marx," fearing the class struggle of Marxism's real practice.[28] The ultimate extension of this was arrived at in Fromm's recent book, *The Revolution of Hope*,[29] wherein he asserts that technology is the main enemy. No longer is the capitalist use of technology the problem, but technology is reified to an absolute position of evil. At approximately the same time, Fromm's political practice revolved around support of the Socialist Party, a reactionary group whose main strength lay in the New York City United Federation of Teachers. The U.F.T.'s racist attacks on black struggles for com-

27 Erich Fromm, *Escape from Freedom* (New York: Holt, 1941), p. 9.
28 Erich Fromm, ed., *Socialist Humanism* (New York: Doubleday).
29 Erich Fromm, *The Revolution of Hope: Toward a Humanized Technology* (New York: Harper & Row, 1968).

munity control apparently did not affect Fromm's politics, and it seems clear that one with such a political practice will be unable to understand the essence of Marxism.

Marcuse's cold war–era *Eros and Civilization* was written in fear of active struggle, and its few political points are couched in psychologisms. Essentially, *Eros* is an attempt to materialize Freudianism by claiming that psychoanalytic theory came out of a scarcity economy and would only achieve its liberating potential when there was a redistribution of wealth. Marcuse takes an orthodox Freudian position, defending the theory of instincts to the point of attacking Fromm and other "revisionists" who felt that the death instinct was a bit much.[30] Marcuse's *Eros,* like Fromm's *Escape,* posits the self-defeat of revolution because of the binds to the oppressor:

> In every revolution, there seems to have been a historical moment when the struggle against domination might have been victorious—but the moment passed. An element of *self-defeat* seems to be involved in this dynamic (regardless of the validity of such reasons as the prematurity and inequality of forces).[31]
>
> Freud's hypothesis of the death instinct and its role in civilized aggression shed light on one of the neglected enigmas of civilization; it revealed the unconscious tie which binds the oppressed to their oppressors, the soldiers to their generals, the individuals to their masters.[32]

This is the extension of instinct theory. Marcuse speaks of, and then discounts, the actual inequality of forces. He instead concentrates on a vision that disre-

30 Herbert Marcuse, *Eros and Civilization: A Philosophical Inquiry into Freud* (Boston: Beacon Press, 1955), p. 249.

31 Ibid., p. 82.

32 Ibid., p. 247.

gards real class struggle as a continuous factor. He even goes a step further—he claims that Freud was pessimistic about the possibilities of humans sublimating their instincts, but that in fact people can do this. So the problem is answered. This is a frightening proposition—it means that Marcuse's "liberation" will involve a large amount of sublimation of human spontaneity and creativity in order to prevent the danger of total freedom. Marcuse is afraid to ask questions about fundamental Freudian principles and therefore becomes an orthodox follower of them, resulting in a backward attitude toward liberation.

Marcuse's later works are more politically oriented, focusing on more realistic problems of revolution, but they still reflect the underlying Freudianism of *Eros*. In his recent book *Counter-Revolution and Revolt* Marcuse speaks of the unity of political and personal liberation, but it is often couched in psychoanalytic terms. For instance, he speaks of the liberation of human nature ("man's primary impulses and senses"),[33] and the aggressive instinct returns to haunt us. Marcuse feels that aggressiveness has been socially steered into technological operations in order to reduce people's guilt. In fact, it is not aggression that has been steered but popular struggle. People are made to feel guilty for their individual problems, for inflation, for war, etc., and it is this guilt that often paralyzes them. An example of this is the collusion of Richard Nixon and George Meany of the A.F.L.-C.I.O. on the 1972–1973 wage freeze: workers are told that their strikes have hurt the American economy and that they must join hands with the bourgeoisie to "strengthen America."

[33] Herbert Marcuse, *Counter-Revolution and Revolt* (Boston: Beacon Press, 1972), p. 59.

Marcuse's cultural critique has never gone far enough to realize the more fundamental question of class oppression and class stratification. This is the logical outcome of a social theory based on Freudian psychology.

The attempt at a Marx-Freud synthesis has even penetrated the minds of revolutionary activists. The popularity of Reimut Reiche among West German revolutionary youth (as well as activists in other parts of Europe and the United States) is a logical extension of the earlier Freudian-Marxian attempts. Reiche's *Sexuality and Class Struggle*[34] contrary to its title, does not speak of class struggle. The book talks about sexuality in modern Western society and provides a Freud-Marx theory of it (with emphasis on Freud). For Reiche "sexual freedom" is a device of capitalist consumerism, a type of "mental manipulation" that has no liberating bases or possibilities.

Reiche traces sexuality through Freudian stages— primitive capitalist accumulation caused the development of an "anal character," and modern consumerist capitalism caused "sexual freedom" to "safeguard" the system. The "anal character" represents a retentive sexuality paralleling a retention of capital in the early phases of accumulation. "Sexual freedom" represents the selling of sexuality in products and services. Now, it is true that early capitalism sought to crush working-class sexuality; that was done as part of the overall social control implemented by the bourgeoisie to stifle human activity and struggle. To speak of the result as an anal character is to mystify it in

[34] Reimut Reiche, *Sexuality and Class Struggle* (London: New Left Books, 1970); for conflicting reviews see Terry Kupers's review and my reply in *Radical Therapist*, vol. 2, no. 4 (December 1971).

psychological terms and to diminish its importance in the total sexual-political-economic repression of the working class. This simplistic and deterministic analysis is the basis for the entire book, resulting in a mystified view of the relationship between sexuality and society. David Fernbach, in a review of the book, pointed out that

> behind Reiche's analysis lies the whole historical distortion of Marxism, as relayed by Lukacs and the Frankfurt School . . . [in which] Class rule is seen as a simple relationship between two constituted groups—capitalists and working class. Politics, ideology, and now sexuality, are only forms through which the class struggle is mediated.[35]

The end result is the subservience of personal liberation to "political" revolution. This has been the result of Stalinism, both in Russia and the United States: struggles for human liberation are considered subordinate to the functionalist bureaucrats and their "plans." Such a revolution holds out self-abnegation to the masses of people instead of showing that the revolution may proceed on many levels simultaneously.

Today, however, the possibilities of liberation are more complete. Marxism has been enriched by many forces—most notably the women's movement—and this transformation enables us to understand and struggle for a unity of political and personal liberation. It has become clear that economic revolution is necessary but not sufficient and that it is definitely possible to create a new society in which people will not live sexually frustrated, power-dominated, competitive lives.

Reiche's solution is to build strong egos and "genital primacy" to fight decadent bourgeois sexuality. He sees homosexuality as an aberration that would "die out" in a "free society," since it is a condition related to the authoritarian personality. His entire book is essentially an orthodox psychoanalytic view of sexuality, with a few modern variations on the theme.

Freudianism arose from the bourgeoisie's counter-revolution against a threatening mass socialist movement; Marxism was born from socialism itself. Their incompatability is precisely the incompatibility of the ruling class and working class. In the hands of certain socialist intellectuals attempts at breaking down this incompatibility lead only to psychologistic mystification of the daily struggles for liberation.

Wilhelm Reich's Marxism held on to a slight amount of psychoanalytic theory, but his radical departure from the conservative orthodoxy of Freudian anthropology brought him far from other Marxist-Freudians. The importance of his work is the subject of the next chapter.

4. Wilhelm Reich and the Sexual-Political Struggle

Wilhelm Reich is best known for his *The Mass Psychology of Fascism,* in which he shows the relationship between sexual repression, family structure, and fascist political rule. In the midst of a growing awareness of psychological oppression and its forcefulness in behavior, Reich's work has become quite important in formulating a new theory of society that encompasses sexuality and personal areas, as well as economic and political forces. Reich tried to work within the German Communist Party to educate its members to the danger of sexual repression, stressing that the party could not achieve true freedom for the masses of people if it did not struggle on the sexual front as well. As had been the case with the socialist movement in the United States, the German workers' movement as a group was as prone to authoritarian sexual attitudes as was the individual person. Reich dared to raise the question of sexual freedom and the problem of repressed sexuality as a block to revolution. For this, the German Communist Party eventually expelled him. To understand fully the importance of Reich's writings it is best to start with his disagreements with psychoanalysis.

REICH VERSUS FREUD

Reich was an early member of the inner group of Freud's followers. His interest in sexology as a medical student led him to see psychoanalysis as a theory and practice that dealt with sexual repression in people. Still a medical student, Reich was accepted openly by Freud and soon was leader of the Technical Seminar, a position second only to that of Freud's.[1]

The closeness between Freud and Reich was not to last very long, however. Early in the game Reich raised objections to Freud's theories. At first these were within the scope of psychoanalysis and for us are unimportant except in that Reich was tending increasingly to recognize sexuality as a more important factor than it was in Freud's view. The real differences began in 1931 as Freud was developing his ideas of society and culture based on psychoanalysis.[2]

In *The Function of the Orgasm,* Reich recounts this argument. He criticizes Freud's reality principle: "Freud neither questioned the irrational in this reality, nor asked which kind of pleasure is compatible with society and which kind is not."[3] Reich goes beyond this point to the dangerous Freudian theory of necessary sublimation of instincts; he says that this subli-

---

[1] The best biographical work is Michel Cattier, *The Life and Work of Wilhelm Reich* (New York: Horizon Press, 1971).

[2] See my chapter on Freud (pages 56–79) for further discussion of this matter.

[3] Wilhelm Reich, *The Function of the Orgasm* (New York: Farrar, Straus & Cudahy, 1961), p. 79.

mation "dams up" life energy and leads to psychic disturbances on both the individual and mass levels.

Reich was at this point working on *Mass Psychology,* which, along with *The Invasion of Compulsory Sex-Morality,* was to become the definitive critique of Freudian anthropology, especially as represented in *Civilization and Its Discontents.* For Reich, the psychoanalytic world view was a preliminary to fascism: "Freud was able to justify the renunciation of happiness on the part of humanity as splendidly as he had defended the fact of infantile sexuality. A few years later, a pathological genius—making the best of human ignorance and fear of happiness—brought Europe to the verge of destruction with the slogan of 'heroic renunciation.' "[4] Freud was maintaining "the unchangeability of human structure as well as of the conditions of human existence."[5] This was becoming clearer as Freud's anthropology progressed. Reich saw that "the function of the suppression of infantile and adolescent sexuality is that of facilitating for the parents the authoritarian submissiveness of the children."[6] While formulating these radical views, Reich was becoming more active in the Communist Party of Austria (this was before he moved to Germany), and revolutionary politics were quite at variance with the reactionary psychoanalytic view of society.

While Reich never fully broke with psychoanalysis or Freud in his own theoretical work, his critique was devastating. In *The Sexual Revolution* Reich speaks of the reality principle as a relative idea, "determined by an authoritarian society," which serves the pur-

4 Ibid., p. 182.
5 Ibid., p. 193.
6 Ibid., p. 195.

poses of that society.[7] He also outlines the major areas that psychoanalysis had "overlooked": that the *unconscious* was socially determined, not an absolute; that the genital gratification spoken of by the psychoanalysts was opposed by all laws and patriarchal religion; that sublimation was only possible in the absence of existing sexual repression; and that capitalist society will not allow the alleviation of sexual repression.[8] Freud's theory of the primal horde is also attacked elsewhere—Reich uses Bronislaw Malinowski's discoveries of the Trobrianders' sexuality to point out the falsities of the theory. He uses evidence of incest relationships among relatives other than mothers and sons, and of the clan-based incest taboo as opposed to Freud's family-based model. And he asks the question that few seem to bother with: how did one horde survive and propagate itself for eons, bearing the same beliefs?[9]

But Reich's reliance on certain Freudian models was strong. Instincts, for instance, were seen as important, although Reich placed them in a social context rather than in a category of innate, absolute behavior. While claiming that psychoanalysis could not be a "world philosophy," Reich was willing to accept it as a partial theory.[10] This failure to understand the fundamental incompatibility of Marxism

---

[7] Wilhelm Reich, The *Sexual Revolution* (New York: Farrar, Straus & Cudahy, 1963), p. 19.

[8] Ibid., p. 19.

[9] Wilhelm Reich, *The Invasion of Compulsory Sex-Morality* (New York: Farrar, Straus & Giroux, 1971), pp. 135–139.

[10] Wilhelm Reich, "Dialectical Materialism and Psychoanalysis," *Studies on the Left,* vol. 6, no. 4 (July–August 1966), pp. 6–17. This essay is now available in Lee Baxandall, ed., *Sex-Pol* (New York: Random House, 1972).

and Freudianism leads to a kind of sexual determinism in Reich's thought, a propensity definitely based on psychoanalysis.

Initially Reich retained certain psychoanalytic ideas of the importance of sexuality in society. In *Mass Psychology* he speaks of Freud's "discovering": (1) "the process that governs psychic life (the unconscious)"; (2) childhood sexuality; (3) the repression of childhood sexuality, especially through the Oedipus complex; and (4) antisexual moral codes as instilled by parents and "parental surrogates" rather than being "of divine origin."[11] These discoveries were in fact Freud's interpretations of real conditions, but in themselves they only served psychoanalysis. Reich was able to locate sexual repression in its historical context and to enrich Marxism with a more total grasp of capitalist social relations. Ultimately, however, sexuality became a moving force for Reich, sometimes overshadowing other important material conditions.

SEXUAL REPRESSION, CAPITALISM, AND FASCISM

For Reich the most dangerous and omnipresent sublimation is that of sexuality, conducted primarily through the family. Representation of the basic life/sexual energy in children leads them to accept this nuclear kernel of authoritarian leadership when they grow up and makes them ripe for fascist types of relationships:

> The interlacing of the socio-economic structure with the sexual structure of society and the structural reproduction of society takes place in the first four or five years and in the authoritarian family. The church only con-

11 Weilhelm Reich, *The Mass Psychology of Fascism* (New York: Farrar, Straus & Giroux, 1970), pp. 26–27.

tinues this function later. Thus, the state gains an enormous interest in the authoritarian family: it becomes the factory in which the state's structure and ideology are molded.[12]

Children for the most part are brought up in sterile atmospheres in which anything sexual is stifled, displaced, or perverted by the parents. Childhood masturbation is punished, although this is becoming increasingly less frequent. "Playing doctor," a euphemism for childhood sexual play, is also punished. In the past the punishment was usually accompanied by false claims about the dangerous results of such activities: blindness, deafness, insanity, impotence, frigidity, God's wrath, etc. Today such "dangers" are hardly credible, but masturbation is still viewed as abnormal in that it supposedly prevents "normal" heterosexual relationships from being a person's sole source of gratification.

Continuous sexual repression makes children fearful, shy, respectful of authority, docile, malleable, afraid of their own sexuality—and therefore afraid of the vital parts of themselves: "Sexual intimidation and inhibition, such as is induced in the child by fear of authority in relation to its thoughts, desires, and sexual acts, make up the core of the psychic structure through which the family conditions the young to Capital."[13]

Reich traces the nuclear patriarchal family through history, mostly using Friedrich Engels's interpretation of Lewis Morgan and J. J. Bachofen.[14] In earlier

[12] Reich, *Mass Psychology,* p. 30.

[13] Wilhelm Reich, *The Sexual Struggle of Youth* (London: Socialist Reproduction, 1972), p. 68.

[14] Friedrich Engels, *The Origin of the Family, Private Property and the State* (New York: International Publishers, 1972).

periods society was matriarchal, with descent through the mother's line. As surplus agricultural products began to accumulate, the males seized power by guarding this surplus, creating the first division of labor, which led to the first social codification of male supremacy. Male supremacy functioned to guarantee identity and transmission of male inheritance, and developed into a system providing free labor from women.

Certain societies are still organized on matriarchal lines. In Trobriand society, for example, sexuality is for the most part not repressed.[15] Other structures within their society also differ greatly from those of patriarchal civilizations, particularly a generalized lack of aggressive behavior.

Patriarchal society, especially in capitalism, serves to bring the power of the state into the family structure:

> For one thing, the political and economic position of the father is reflected in his patriarchal relationship to the remainder of the family. In the figure of the father the authoritarian state has its representative in every family, so that the family becomes its most important instrument of power. . . . What this position of the father actually necessitates is the strictest sexual suppression of the women and children.[16]

All the values of the society as a whole are transmitted through the family, with emphasis on the moral

---

[15] Reich's *Compulsory Sex-Morality* is nearly entirely a presentation of Malinowski's *Sexual Life of Savages* and is very important for understanding this area. Reich plays down the fact that there is a ruling clique and that those children destined to be part of it are sexually suppressed. It is unclear how important this is, however, in terms of the overall differences between matriarchy and patriarchy.

[16] Reich, *Mass Psychology*, p. 53.

areas, especially sexuality. The family structure mystifies it, with legends, myths, etc.: motherhood is identified with national greatness, as well as the Virgin
Mary; the father is identified as the god figure; the
family is considered the building block of the nation.
(Nazism especially utilized these myths, making them
a major propaganda tool.) Masturbation is punishable
by God, who sees it even when the parents don't.
Combined with religion, "organized mysticism" is
profoundly antisexual and is a powerful agent in
bringing fascism to the masses.[17]

There is little possibility of a child escaping this
social, economic, political, and religious army of sexual repression. Acceptance of the status quo is a
logical outcome of such training. Since the child cannot fend for him/herself—this is part of the training—he/she must remain in the family nexus and
submit to parental repression. It is only in the past
decade or so, and primarily in the United States, that
teenagers leave home before marriage. Prior to this
there was no way for them to survive economically or
to overcome the social disapproval brought about by
such behavior. Even these teenagers, however, are
already conditioned by their parents and other institutions. They have learned to be afraid of their bodies
and of sexuality. Even in today's so-called sexual
revolution we encounter the same attitudes, especially
the oppression of women by men (to whom society
allows almost unlimited sexual gratification).

Sexuality is mystified in so many ways that children are not even aware of what questions to ask
in order to liberate their sexuality. Thus, whereas the
average person is inclined from social conditioning to

[17] Ibid., pp. 56, 115–169.

accept authoritarian society, he is even more inclined to accept outright fascism, since the same mystification is extolled. For instance, Nazism embraced ascetic ideals, the sublimity of motherhood, and female subservience—all in a mystical way, tied to Germanic mythology and cosmogony.[18] This mysticism, in the absence of the possibility of asking questions or establishing logical ways of thinking, has the power to captivate the masses of people who succumb to what Reich called the "emotional plague." Reich did not discount Marxist materialism as an explanation for the rise of Nazism, but he has given us much material to show how the internalization of sexual repression also played a major factor.

INTERNALIZATION AND MARXISM

Reich's analysis of the internalization of repression is a major point in contemporary revolutionary Marxism. Like Rosa Luxemburg and Antonio Gramsci, Reich realized that Marxism meant more than economic determinism. He developed in *Mass Psychology* the theory that ideology, initially a response to material conditions, waxes so strong that it becomes a material force itself.

Internalized repression is the most difficult type to detect and to combat, since it is seen as a "natural" way. Sexual morality is not the only internalized morality, but it is probably the most prominent. Histories of sexuality and sex education can tell little compared to

[18] Louis Pauwels and Jacques Bergier, in *The Morning of the Magicians* (New York: Avon, 1968), discuss mythology and cosmogony in Nazi Germany. Although their framework is not akin to mine, the points they raise about this matter are very informative. See also *Mass Psychology*, pp. 85, 93–96, for Reich's views of Nazi mythology.

our own everyday observations: that aspect of youthful freedom most threatening to parents is sexuality. The archaic laws on sex, abortion, and contraception are clearly designed to prevent natural sexual relations. In states like New York and Massachusetts the power of the Catholic Church is so strong that it functions as a more powerful antisexual force than the legislatures. But the church doesn't have a monopoly on such attitudes—there is mass support for the institutional repression of sexuality.

Counterculture institutions are tolerated in this society unless they deal with sexuality—a woman's health center in Los Angeles was raided by the police, who jailed several women for showing other women how to treat their own vaginal infections.[19] Many people have been jailed for giving advice on contraception and abortion, and a woman in Florida was even jailed for having had an abortion. At demonstrations women typically encounter aggressive sexual remarks from the cops, and men are called fags. The same attitudes are displayed in schools, hospitals, and other institutions. Sexual activity among prisoners and mental patients is looked upon as threatening behavior. Sometimes it is tolerated to cool them out, but most of the time it causes extension of their sentences.

How does internalized repression become so powerful? Reich speaks of the power of cultural dominance, quoting Marx: "In every epoch the ideas of the ruling class are the ruling ideas, i.e., the class which is the ruling material power of the society also constitutes that society's ideological power."[20] The familial training mentioned above is the most forceful and

---

[19] *Rough Times,* vol. 3, no. 3 (December 1972), p. 21.
[20] Karl Marx, *The German Ideology* (New York: International Publishers, 1969).

effective form of repression. It leads to situations like popular support for World War I—the millions of anti-imperialists in European workers' parties were quick to support their nation either through apathy or the "clear martial enthusiasm" that was psychically instilled in them.[21] Similarly, the officer is feared, says Reich, because he is a father figure.[22] Reich considers the internalization so powerful that the masses desire a führer to tell them—in a fatherly manner—what to do.[23]

> The revolutionary movement also failed to appreciate the importance of the seemingly irrelevant everyday habits, indeed, very often turned them to bad account. The lower middle-class bedroom suite, which the "rabble" buys as soon as he has the means, even if he is otherwise revolutionary minded; the consequent suppression of the wife, even if he is a Communist; the "decent" suit of clothes for Sunday; "proper" dance steps and a thousand other "banalities," have an incomparably greater reactionary influence when repeated day after day than thousands of revolutionary rallies and leaflets can ever hope to counterbalance. Narrow conservative life exercises a continuous influence, penetrates every facet of everyday life; whereas factory work and revolutionary leaflets have only a brief effect. Thus, it was a grave mistake to cater to the conservative tendencies in the workers by giving banquets "as a means of getting at the masses."[24]

The same situation can be observed in virtually all aspects of our everyday lives: working-class and lower-middle-class people struggling hard in order to buy a house in the "right" part of town, upholding those

21 Reich, *Mass Psychology,* pp. 22–23. Reich doesn't discount the failure of the left parties but maintains that these factors were equally important.
22 Ibid., p. 32.
23 Ibid., pp. 218, 281.
24 Ibid., p. 69.

bourgeois ethics that are the same as those used to crush them at other times; the examples are infinite. Some socialists today also present attitudes similar to the ones that were behind the banquets Reich speaks of—one example is anticommunal living and anti-marijuana beliefs, which are aimed at "reaching the workers," etc.

Often one hears arguments that consider internalized repression to be in reality a survival tactic, a way of living in an oppressive environment. Certainly this is partially the case, as is the case with women who are forced to wear certain clothes and makeup to work and behave "properly." There are, though, innumerable situations in which survival is not at stake and people's bourgeois thinking and behavior remain intact.

Internalization is everywhere, all the time. Most examples of it have changed little since Reich's time—only the outward appearances change, if even those. In general, internalization of sociosexual repression has not been considered an important enough factor in people's failure to oppose fascism. A whole nation supported Nazism almost instantaneously, countless Italian Communist Party members joined the Fascist Party, the United States as a nation supports genocide in Vietnam and elects by overwhelming support a president pledged to continue that genocide. Many believe that this is simply a matter of the people not having access to true information and to their having nothing to gain by opposing the reaction. Many believe that only industrial workers will lead the revolution, that the revolution will revolve around economic matters and to raise issues of a noneconomic nature would be faulty. Unfortunately, as Reich was fought by the German Communist Party, so too those who raise similar issues are fought here by the Stalinist "left." It becomes difficult to speak of repressed and internalized sexuality or internalization, since most people are afraid of confronting this in themselves.

The failure of economism (reliance on simple bread-and-butter issues) in organizing large numbers of people is apparent—the organizer typically fails to relate to the whole person. He doesn't understand that people want change in more than their work place relations. Today it is clear that the material factors creating a revolutionary climate are greater than simply economic factors. The way people live, whom they live with, and their visions of a better life are as tangible as the assembly line on which they toil. Reich attempted to organize somewhat along these lines in Sex-Pol.

SEX-POL

Little is known of the actual workings of the Sex-Pol organization. Reich organized it by recruiting members of a sexual reform association, as well as young Communists with whom he was working. Adding to the problems of sexual repression in families, party cells were also restricting sexuality. Youth had no place to go to have sexual relations, even within party organizations. Sex-Pol provided counseling for youths troubled by their sex lives, encouraging them to engage in sexual relations as long as those relations were free and nonoppressive.

Literature and lectures provided information on contraception, abortion, venereal disease, and the social-political nature of human sexuality. Sex-Pol demanded free distribution of safe contraceptive devices; complete abolition of antiabortion legislation; free abortion on demand; two months' paid pregnancy leave, before and after confinement; abolition of all compulsory regulations of marriage and divorce; abolition of prostitution by attacking its causes: "unemployment, dual sexual morality, and the ideology of abstinence"; abolition of venereal disease through mass preventive measures and free clinics; public clinics to help people with sexual problems; abolition of laws on and punishments for victimless crimes involving sex. Sex-Pol knew that "it must be clearly recognized that the manifesto cannot be fulfilled within the capitalist state" and that the organization had to show people how sex-political struggle linked up to other mass struggles.[25]

From its inception in 1926 the Sex-Pol movement attempted to work with the Communist Party in addition to sexual reform organizations. Sex-Pol's major printed work, *The Sexual Struggle of Youth*,[26] was in fact supposed to be published by the party. This book provided basically accurate (for that era) information on sexual biology, contraception, abortion, and venereal disease, as well as presenting in easy fashion the sex-political theories of Reich. *Sexual Struggle* fell prey to Reich's antihomosexuality and male supremacy attitudes, but as a whole it was quite a revolutionary publication. For the Communist Party it was too

[25] "History of the German Sex-Pol Group," in Wilhelm Reich and Karl Teschitz, *Selected Sex-Pol Essays, 1934–1937* (London: Socialist Reproduction, 1973), pp. 48–49. This is an invaluable book of previously untranslated articles from the Sex-Pol journal. For publisher's address, see Bibliography.

[26] The only complete English-language edition is available from Socialist Reproduction (London, 1973). The final chapter, "Politisizing the Sexual Problems of Youth," is reprinted in Wilhelm Reich, *Sex-Pol,* ed. Lee Baxandall (New York: Random House, 1972).

revolutionary—they withdrew their support from it, and from that point on they acted more and more hostilely to Sex-Pol. The Party's attitude reflected the sexual crisis then occurring in the Soviet Union, which Reich understood in part. Further, the Party line opposed Sex-Pol's willingness to work with Social-Democratic youths.

Youth communes in Russia were experimenting with new forms of living and working but typically encountered obstacles in their own sexual unfreedom. Reich speaks of this in *The Sexual Revolution*, mentioning the youth communes' asceticism, antiabortion beliefs, and lack of respect for privacy. In part this was a response to power-related sex in revolutionary Russia—including a certain amount of prostitution. But beyond that, it was also a part of the "sex negative" character that Reich saw in the U.S.S.R., a character that would a few years later reinstitute repressive laws on homosexuality and tighten up marriage and divorce procedures. The Soviet Union clearly fit the pattern of what Reich had been speaking of all along—Stalinism's political repression necessitated sexual repression to stifle the self-consciousness that had been developing among the youth of Russia.

Reich's influence in Marxist circles was negligible for many years after the early 1930s. This was most likely due to a combination of his pursuit of orgone theory, his growing political cynicism, and the failure of a sexual revolution (or any other kind of revolution) in Russia. Current transformation in Marxist theory and practice has brought Reich to light, offering his guidelines on how to approach a total revolution. At present an understanding of Reich's perspective on economic-political-sexual repression and their workings in capitalist society is of immense importance in formulating a Marxist psychology. Not only can this perspective give people a clearer idea of what communism would look like, but it also enables organizers to rethink old tactics and learn new ways of approaching the totality of people's daily oppression.

5. Frantz Fanon: Psychology and Revolution

Frantz Fanon, born in the French colony of Martinique, provides major insights for the development of a Marxist psychology. Since he is read more by revolutionaries than by psychologists and psychiatrists, he is usually perceived as a figure in revolutionary history rather than as a contributor to a liberating psychology. Writing from his experience in colonized Algeria, Fanon tells us in broad terms that most of "mental illness" is caused by the social system and can be removed by changing that system. His position is usually considered simplistic by those who cannot accept a total view of society. Detractors of this sort are not seeing the world in the dialectical terms that Fanon utilizes—they live in a world of compartmentalized ideas in which politics and psychology never come together. This compartmentalization is an agent of mystification, and Fanon embarks on a course of breaking it down.

One of the most severe problems he saw among the

Algerians was "autodestruction." In *The Wretched of the Earth* he states that colonial oppression

> keeps alive in the native an anger which he deprives of outlet; the native is trapped in the tight links of the chains of colonialism. But we have seen inwardly the settler can only achieve a pseudo-petrification. The native's muscular tension finds outlets regularly in bloodthirsty explosion—in tribal warfare, in feuds between sects, and in quarrels between individuals.[1]

It is the powerlessness of the colonized with regard to the ruler which makes him attack his brothers and sisters rather than his master. Eldridge Cleaver has written that the same can be seen in the ghettos of the United States.

In *Black Skin, White Masks* Fanon examines the Martiniquans' attempts to become "French," an attempt that he made at one time. The result of his attempt was that he became a psychiatrist and lost identification with his oppressed comrades. But being a black psychiatrist in Algeria in the middle of the Algerian revolution changed many things. The identification with the oppressor that for so long was a major part of the oppressed life began to change, and energy flowed in revolutionary directions.

Fanon also sees the displacement of aggression (an aggression that, when directed toward the colonialists, is good) in the myth and magic which occupy such a large part of the colonized people's life. The zombies become "more terrifying than the settlers," and thus the colonialists' power is effectively reduced in the mind of the Algerian. Another psychological trap is the acceptance of colonialist psychology, specifically the "complexes": the "frustration complex," the

[1] Frantz Fanon, *The Wretched of the Earth* (New York: Grove Press, 1968), p. 43.

"belligerency complex," the "colonizability complex," the "laziness complex," and so on, ad infinitum. This internalization of oppression is, in the earlier stages of colonialism, often too subtle to detect. It is very similar to the myths we in the United States accept about ourselves—until we are aware of the possibilities of liberation, we believe or half believe the ruler and/or psychiatrist who tells us that our rebellion against parents or teachers is due to an unresolved complex.

Internalization of oppression leads to a general cultural-social consciousness that various people have called "mass neurosis" (Fromm) or "emotional plague" (Reich). The process of history in the unliberated era leads to the all-pervasive and nonconscious acceptance of one's own inferiority and powerlessness in a world controlled by others. Similar to Reich, Fanon describes the familial and sexual repression that cripples people, preventing them from struggling for freedom. These deep-seated aspects of consciousness are harder to fight against than are the more "acute" emotional crises with which the psychiatrist is usually concerned. Fanon could have helped the "acute" patients, but he didn't consider that as an answer, for "the circumstances of the cured patients maintain and feed these pathological kinks." That is, going back into the same world of oppression is bound to re-create the initial problems, and Fanon sees revolution as the agent of change: "The colonized man finds his freedom in and through violence." Fanon quotes from Aimé Césaire's *Les armes miraculeuses,* in which the slave strikes the master: "I struck, the blood flowed: that is the only *baptism* that I remember today."[2]

---

[2] Frantz Fanon, *Black Skin, White Masks* (New York: Grove Press, 1967), p. 198.

Is this revolutionary violence cathartic? Only in the sense that it represents the essence of the national liberation struggle, that it gives the colonized power over her/his own life for the first time. This doesn't mean that killing a French person rids the Algerian of all her/his problems, nor does it imply that the National Liberation Front (F.L.N.) triumph was a solution to all emotional problems. Fanon is simply the first person to say that emotional problems or "mental illness" or whatever one calls them cannot be totally alleviated in the context of an oppressive society. This may seem too simple, and in fact, there are drawbacks. The Algerians threw out the French but didn't attain real revolution: on one hand, socialist forces were beaten back by national bourgeoisie; on the other, full cultural liberation was not achieved.

Fanon was concerned with more than just a political revolution against the French colonialists. He saw that cultural liberation was part of the revolutionary upsurge. This included the breaking down of traditional Algerian patriarchy, under which the father reigned supreme over his household. Youths were unable to accept parental authority while they were in the revolutionary forces; women refused their subservient role of near slavery. The revolutionary situation created, out of immediate necessity, various changes in sex roles and family authority. Fanon hoped that these, and other aspects of cultural liberation, would continue, but the national bourgeoisie's seizure of control put an end to that process.

The more Fanon understood about the totality of the Algerian revolution, the more he clarified his definition of a revolutionary psychology. From his Marxist perspective on the totality of colonial domination, it was logical that he would understand how the psychology ascribed by Europeans to Africans was another aspect of that domination. The French made no pretense of applying the same psychology to Algerians as to French. The totality of French racism—political, sexual, economic—was simply transformed into a codified psychology that explained away the primary fact of imperialism.

With the totality of imperialist oppression on their backs, the colonized discover their own totality: "The native discovers reality and transforms it into the pattern of his customs, into the practice of violence and into his plans for freedom."[3] There is no longer a separation of racist psychology from racist violence. Psychology has been discovered as part of the entire system of exploitation, and a new psychology must arise to take its place: a psychology of freedom.

Fanon stands as the most complete synthesizer of psychology and political struggle. It is not an artificial synthesis but a dialectical one that understands the unity of these two aspects of human praxis. Through Fanon's writings, it is possible to know how psychology arises from political struggle, and vice versa. He also provides a method by which to understand the complexity of what capitalism does to people's lives. And out of necessity Fanon leads us to knowing why we create a revolution. Violence is demystified as it becomes clearly a violence begun by the rulers. There is no longer a need for creating a radical psychology; rather there is the real necessity of engaging in the revolutionary struggle that will create the new psychology.

---

[3] Fanon, *Wretches of the Earth*, p. 46.

6. Antipsychiatry

Antipsychiatry—the work mainly of R. D. Laing, Aaron Esterson, and David Cooper—is a critical point in Marxist psychology. Others such as Mary Barnes, Joe Berke, and Morton Schatzman receive little attention, but the totality of antipsychiatry overturns so much of traditional psychology that we must study it carefully.

On the surface, what do we get? Severe questioning of the very concept of mental illness, and the beginnings of a new world view. This new approach *politicizes* psychology and draws out the hidden power and ideology which has hitherto been masked by fancy words.

A generation of young people have R. D. Laing as one of their gurus; *The Politics of Experience* continues to be a best-selling book and increasingly is being used in straight college courses. The question, Who is crazier, the person who feels he/she has an A-bomb inside him/herself, or the person with the power to drop the bomb? is typical of the antipsychiatric approach. This sort of question is being raised for the first time, and now can begin to be answered.

ORIGINS IN EXISTENTIALISM

Antipsychiatry began with Laing's attempt to create a masterpiece of existential psychology in *The Divided Self*. Picking up from the European existential/phenomenological tradition (especially Ludwig Binswanger), Laing's purpose was "to make madness, and the process of going mad, comprehensible. . . . A further purpose is to give in plain English an account in existential terms of some forms of madness."[1]

Laing's existentialism was a stated opposition to the false schemes of classification of mental illness and to the mystifying activities of most professions. The new view of the person was to locate that person in-the-world, not solely in-the-psyche. This contradicted the prevailing attitudes, which yielded "a common illusion that one somehow increases one's understanding of a person if one can translate a personal understanding of him into the impersonal terms of a sequence or system of it-processes."[2]

Laing's liberation of psychology from power-defined categories located sanity as a social construct rather than a medical illness: "I suggest, therefore, that sanity or psychosis is tested by the degree of conjunction or disjunction between two persons where the one is sane by common consent."[3] This position asserted that "granting" sanity or insanity to a person

---

[1] R. D. Laing, *The Divided Self*, (New York: Pantheon, 1970).
[2] Ibid., p. 22.
[3] Ibid., p. 26.

was based on establishment authority concerning sanity.

Laing follows with the criteria of sanity versus insanity. Sanity will be determined by "ontological security," insanity by "ontological insecurity," "ontological" referring to a person's existence, his being. The ontologically secure person

> may experience his own being as real, alive and whole; as differentiated from the rest of the world in ordinary circumstances so clearly that his identity and autonomy are never in question; as a continuum in time; as having an inner consistency, substantiality, genuineness and worth; as spatially coextensive with the body and usually as having begun in or around birth and liable to extinction with death.[4]

The ontologically insecure person

> in the ordinary circumstances of living may feel more unreal than real; in a literal sense more dead than alive; precariously differentiated from the rest of the world, so that his identity and autonomy are always in question. He may lack the experience of his temporal continuity. He may not possess an overriding sense of personal consistency and cohesiveness. He may feel more insubstantial than substantial, and unable to assume that the stuff he is made of is genuine, good, valuable. And he may feel his self as partially divorced from his body.[5]

Adding to these definitions, Laing speaks of "implosion," "petrification," and "engulfment," all essentially psychiatric terms for modes of experiencing one's self. The picture is still, therefore, bound by specific problems of personality structure in individuals; but Laing is able to begin explaining what splits people feel in their lives.

[4] Ibid., pp. 41–42.
[5] Ibid., p. 42.

Take, for example, Laing's discussion of the case of Julie. Julie refers to herself as "Mrs. Taylor," and Laing analyzes this as her attempt to express that she feels "tailor-made, a tailored maid, made, fed, clothed, tailored."[6] For Laing this is a cryptic world, but the crypticness masks the real pain. Julie experiences herself as being treated in these ways and has no path out of her life, so she lives in a metaphorical fantasy that has a real basis in her family life.[7]

Laing's metaphorical descriptions and analyses of psychoses were important advances over past models, for there was some amount of personal characterization. The patient was seen in context, but that context was too narrow, without regard to a dialectical-materialist viewpoint. Thus, much of *Divided Self* is based on the "self-body split," in which the traditional dualism of mind and body comes out of its hiding place.

Yet Laing is already speaking of a basic failure to understand the schizophrenic and pushing his position that we ought to understand people in his existential terms. Well, there is no doubt that many of Laing's descriptions of the context of symptoms hold their own, but the Laingian model is not sufficient as a total explanation of personal behavior. One reason is the failure to locate these events in a more material world, using the metaphorical models as a mainstay of the analysis. Another reason is that Laing sees much of this understanding being done only by the therapist.[8]

A further danger is that behavior under the doctor's

---

[6] Ibid., p. 192.

[7] This discussion of Julie is based partly on an unpublished manuscript by Keith Brooks and Phil Brown, "The Revolt against Psychology."

[8] Ibid., p. 165.

scrutiny is liable to be invalid. Laing in fact shows how traditional psychiatry drives people to couch their perceptions of reality so that the doctor will not retaliate:

A good deal of schizophrenic activity is simply non-sense, red-herring speech, prolonged filibustering to throw dangerous people off the scent, to create boredom and futility in others. The schizophrenic is often making a fool of himself and the doctor. He is playing at being mad to avoid at all costs the possibility of being held responsible for a single coherent idea, or intention.[9]

Such protection surely is not restricted to mad people. Laing's awareness of protective devices used by all people comes through his insistence that life is quite dangerous in this society: "In a world full of danger, to be a potentially seeable object is to be constantly exposed to danger. Self-consciousness, then, may be the apprehensive awareness of oneself as potentially exposed to danger by the simple fact of being visible to others. The obvious defense against such a danger is to make oneself invisible in one way or another.[10] This shows Laing's awareness of the dangers, but the world he sees in *Divided Self* is still mainly existential, without any materiality. Self-consciousness, as he speaks of it, could better be termed knowing your real self in a world where that is prohibited, or knowing one's own oppression.

For all of Laing's shortcomings *Divided Self* was a major breakthrough in establishing a phenomenologically oriented world view. Yet it was the culmination of the classic existential psychology tradition—Laing had taken Binswanger to the limits and come up with a radical new approach. It was not possible to go

[9] Ibid., p. 164.
[10] Ibid., p. 109.

further without adding the material world, especially in Marxist terms; however, the introduction of Marxism to antipsychiatry was still a few years away. For the intervening period Laing's antipsychiatry concentrated on the family.

In early antipsychiatry one's mental illness was only incidentally discussed in relation to one's family environment. As it moved ahead, antipsychiatry would focus primarily on the family. Laing's *The Self and Others*[11] is the first place where he speaks of the family to any extent, although only incidentally. Laing was developing a theory of interpersonal communication that may seem to show a sharp rupture with the clinical nature of *Divided Self*. It has become clear, however, that the two books were probably written at the same time and intended to be complementary to each other.[12]

THE FAMILY

In speaking of fantasy systems as ways people have of relating to certain situations, Laing began to observe this in the family. Fantasy is essentially a mode of experiencing that is seen as unreal by the arbiters of reality. In the family the child feels oppressed by the actual (real) structure of the family. Thus she/he relates to the world (family world and/or total world) in an independent way (fantasy, hallucination, etc.) that the socializing family cannot bear. This framework of Laing's is useful but needs to be expanded. The family (like other institutions in capitalist so-

[11] R. D. Laing, *The Self and Others* (New York: Pantheon, 1961).

[12] This idea is based on similarities in the two books, as well as on recent allusions to it by Laing.

ciety) mystifies the real world of the child (person). It channels life energy into restricted patterns of thought and action.

There are different levels of fantasy: (1) the child's independent view of the world and (2) the family's own fantasy, which arises from its own mystifying processes. This latter level is the family's response to the world around it, whereas the former is the result of the family's attempt to prevent the child from knowing the "reality" from which the family has "escaped."

For fear of lettting the "secret" out, the family fantasy must be *real-ized* (made to seem real) so that no one can be in the position of creating *independent* fantasies. So for the child, the family is presenting the familial fantasy as reality, which in effect is the family reality as fantasy. The matter works both ways, and the dialectical interaction of these two paths typically leads to a confused state of mind for the child (or other person in the middle of the situation). For instance, a family has a fantasy that they arc a "happy family," that they do not fight and hassle all the time. In fact, this is not the case, but the fantasy is held up to the child (and the outside world) as the reality of life. When the child sees that this is not reality, the parents mask and mystify the conflicts. For the child this means that she cannot say too much to the parents about the situation, for she will then blow their cover and they will take it out on her.

Where the fantasy mode could be creating new possibilities, there is at every step a constraint against pursuing fantasies for fear of losing the individual's subservience to the social order. Thus the family is forced on the child as a positive reality. Fantasy was seen by Laing as a way of relating to untenable situations, and the family began to appear to be the prime example of such a situation. The family counters the autonomy of the child's fantasy by pressing upon the child the parental fantasy: i.e., that the family is *real*. Of course, the family *is* real in that it exists as a major part of people's lives. *The fantasy of the family* consists of the false trust and of the belief in the family's omniscience and omnipotence and goodness which is inculcated in the family members. *The monstrous mystification of the family as the only reality is what becomes the fantasy of the family*.

Much of what is called fantasy is, in fact, doing for *others* instead of for *oneself*. All of the child's activities must fit into the family's life. Thus the child must *pretend* to *do* things, when in fact he is having these things *done to* him. Having been defined as a *being-for-others* instead of a *being-for-self*, the child must be careful not to be too much of his own self. Laing explains this in terms of play. The child must *learn* to play: "In childhood, if one does not succeed in playing not to be playing when one is playing at being 'simply oneself,' very soon they will get worried about infantile omnipotence going on far too long."[13] So even to be oneself, one must pretend not to be.

As an example, take a child who is playing with a cooking pan. If the child is a boy, the parents will most likely not see this play as "play-cooking" and will ask the boy what he's doing. But the child, happy to be playing with the pan as an object for play, has no answer, since there is no answer. This scares the parents, for the child does not fit into a "normal" play routine, and in fact, is asserting his independence to play as he chooses, with or without a game or goal. If

13 Laing, *Self and Others*, p. 32.

play is free, play for itself, the child and his parents obviously have a different idea of what is going on—and the child is in trouble if he does not figure out how to pretend otherwise. Further, this boy is not learning the appropriate sex role and so threatens the ingrained attitudes (and eventually the actual operations of the family as primary socializer).

A mass image of this is: "Where are you going?" "Out." "What are you doing?" "Nothing." Life itself has become threatening, so these answers are given whether or not the parent will actually rebuke the child. The child has been so confused that he no longer understands what is permissible; therefore he develops a protection that can ultimately lead to total noncommunication and land him in the hospital.

Antipsychiatry was beginning to understand being-for-others but became bogged down in seeing otherness in terms of arbitrary structures—the child was being-for-others, but there was little explication of who the others were. Were the others simply the parents, or the outside world, the "real" world? Without understanding capitalist society's channeling of human behavior for its own needs, psychology could not adequately explain the roots of family repression. Laing was dealing with categories of the *self* and *others,* and this led to a position taken by antipsychiatry, a position of *structuralism,* in which social structures are seen as definite, mechanical, and ahistorical (always existing, regardless of the context), not changeable by human praxis and material circumstances.[14]

The structures dealt with are real in the sense that they reflect the situations in which people usually find

[14] This is not to label Laing a structuralist but to emphasize his vulnerability to this orientation.

themselves. Such things as families and factories, schools and sexual relations, are *real;* they certainly have their own structures. But these structures do not define the institutional workings or the capacities for the structures/institutions to change. *Structures change with history; they cannot explain history.* Laing was falling into the pattern of seeing family authority as a thing in itself, without any real examples of the parents' roles in the rest of society. Parental authority does not simply exist; it consists of bringing to a certain social unit the authority of the whole society. The child fights back not simply because of a structuralist notion that all children fight back but because the child's autonomy and existence are deeply threatened. The "rebellious" child is a mystified concept—children are not innately rebellious but rebel for real reasons and with real behavior.

There is not simply a system of family structures but rather an *arena of conflict.* The conflict arises out of the different power positions of the parents and children and especially in the parents' class origins and how those origins affect their own psyches. Often the conflict is over the acceptance of male or female behavior patterns, but this important area is not delved into by Laing. Laing does know, however, that we can observe the power relations. Take this example:

> During direct observation of the relationship between a six-month-old child and its mother, the occasions in which smiling occurred were noted. It was observed, first of all, that infant and mother smiled at each other not infrequently. It was then further observed that the mother, during the periods of observation, never once responded with a smile to the infant's initial smile at her. She, however, evoked smiling in the infant by smiling herself, by tickling and playing with the infant.

> When she was the evoker of the infant's smiles, she in
> turn smiled back, but she responded with a flat, dull
> look if the infant took the initiative.[15]

Must we not ask how the mother was trained to bring
up children; how this pattern was visible in other
facets of her life? It is likely that the same one-sided
smiling communications system exists between her
and her husband. The same is true of workers and
bosses, but we must remember that the problem is not
communication but rather the *power* behind this communication. Communication simply expresses the
power relations between people and is bound to be
faulty when class conflict or family conflict is involved.

A further example of Laing's failure to transcend
structures completely is his discussion of *collusion:* "a
'game' played by two or more people whereby they
deceive themselves" and in which "an essential feature of this game is not admitting that it is a game."[16]
If we accept the earlier definitions of fantasy and false-
self systems, it is difficult to accept the equality of
collusion. Laing admits that it is difficult in practice to
determine the extent of collusion, though he adds that
the point is "worth making theoretically." And fortu-
nately, he speaks later of further complexities—especially forced behavior, which is demanded to
complement the identity of the powerful person. Laing
sees certain ramifications of this: "If one refuses
collusion, one feels guilt for not being or not becoming the embodiment of the complement demanded by
the other for his identity. However if one *does* suc-

[15] Laing, *Self and Others,* p. 85, quoted from W. M.
Bradley, "Some Family Operations and Schizophrenia," *AMA
Archives of General Psychiatry* (1959): 379.
[16] Laing, *Self and Others,* p. 90.

cumb, if one is seduced, one becomes estranged from one's self and is guilty thereby of self-betrayal."[17] This is certainly the way such an operation functions, but it is necessary to explore the actual bases of power that some people have over others.

Power is more clearly defined in Laing's discussion of the *double-bind,* a basic occurrence in the nuclear family. He gives an example of a mother visiting her son, who is recovering from a "nervous breakdown." She opens her arms for him to embrace her but stiffens as he gets nearer. He stops, and she accuses him of not wanting to embrace her. Obviously she does not really want affection from her child (or is in conflict about it) but is playing at wanting it. So she declines to follow through; he responds as best he can, whereupon she accuses him of not loving her. *He cannot win no matter what he does.* There are innumerable other examples. The classic one is of one man asking another, "Do you still beat your wife?" A positive answer means present guilt; a negative answer means past guilt. There is no way out. The way out is closed by the *phrasing* of the question, which then defines the answers.[18] Although Laing still views double-bind as a communications failure, he knows it is present in the basic family unit. In moving along, antipsychiatry began to focus more clearly on the daily occurrence of double-bind, as well as other family patterns.

Sanity, Madness and the Family, written by Laing and Aaron Esterson in 1964, was the result of years

[17] Ibid., p. 93.
[18] The double-bind theory was originally formulated in Bateson, Jackson, Haley, and Weakland, "Towards a Theory of Schizophrenia," *Behavioral Science,* 1 (1956): 251, and reprinted in Gregory Bateson, *Steps toward an Ecology of Mind* (New York: Ballantine, 1972).

of study of "schizophrenic" women and their families. The roots of youth's problems—particularly identity, autonomy, sexuality—were outlined more specifically. There was, however, a tendency to see the family as the absolute structure that determined people's emotional problems. The family was somewhat separated from the outside world, and an understanding of the basis of its roles and functioning remained to be reached.

Looking at *Sanity, Madness and the Family,* we find clear examples of parental collusion and real bases for "paranoia" on the child's part. Sarah Danzig, considered paranoid, "hallucinated" about her mail being intercepted and her phone calls being monitored by her parents. Investigating her family, Laing and Esterson found that these were, in fact, real features of her life. There were also any number of instances of collusion between father and mother, mother and brother, etc., in which Sarah was the victim. Sarah's parents spoke of her illness as centered around her attempts to discuss forbidden issues (forbidden by her parents), her angry responses to her family's mystification of common experience, and her constant attempts to open up the family's secrecy on any number of issues.[19] Laing and Esterson found that Sarah's fears were completely founded on truth and that her behavior was totally intelligible in light of her parents' actions. They do not examine the parents' behavior deeply, however, and we are left only with the Danzigs's seemingly irrational actions. This unfortunately doesn't explain why Mr. and Mrs. Danzig behave as they do.[20]

[19] R. D. Laing and Aaron Esterson, *Sanity, Madness and the Family* (New York: Basic Books, 1965), pp. 109–130.

[20] Esterson attempts to go further in his more recent *The Leaves of Spring,* discussed later.

Esterson and Laing understood their limitations. In describing the incomplete nature of their "totalization" of the family, they note that "the focus remains somewhat on the identified patient, or on the mother-daughter relationship, on the person-in-a-nexus rather than on the nexus itself. This we believe to be historically unavoidable.[21] Indeed it was unavoidable—Laing and Esterson had yet to outline a method that would explain the deeper complexities. Still, they had broken many traditions: "We believe that the shift of point of view that these descriptions both embody and demand has a historical significance no less radical than the shift from a demonological to a clinical viewpoint three hundred years ago."[22] The necessary method would have to provide a better synthesis of social context and individual psychology, of existentialism and Marxism, and of subjective and objective. It arrived soon, based on Sartre's Marxism.

PHENOMENOLOGY AND MARXISM

Reason and Violence is an explication of Sartre's *Search for a Method, Saint Genêt,* and *Critique de la Raison Dialectique.* Its purpose is to make Sartre's ideas intelligible in brief form, especially as the *Critique* has not as yet been translated into English. What is given us is Sartre's method of combining existentialism and Marxism, the former being conditional upon the latter. Philosophy expresses the social context, serving as a "cultural milieu for the men of that time."[23] There are three "moments" of the

[21] Laing and Esterson, *Sanity, Madness and the Family,* p. 26.

[22] Ibid., p. 27.

[23] R. D. Laing and David Cooper, *Reason and Violence* (New York: Barnes & Noble, 1964), p. 31.

Sartrean method: (1) *phenomenological description,* or observation by experience, though based on some general theory; (2) *the analytico-regressive moment,* "a regression backward into the history of the object to define and date its earlier stages"; and (3) *the synthetic-progressive moment,* which "moves from past to present in an attempt to rediscover the present.[24]

It is this dialectical process that can provide both a phenomenal and a material analysis of human behavior, relating behavior to real events in light of their history. To create the dialectical explanations for the three moments, *totalization* is employed, the grasping of a social reality in the context of all social influences around it, the effect of the people within it, and the dialectical relations between the people and the situations. Totalizations are constantly retotalized to incorporate all new changes, as well as possible changes, thus constituting an eternal dialectic.[25]

Also of importance is *intention:* "Critical experience cannot be established without its own intention, namely the perpetual reorganization of the given in terms of acts illumined by their ends."[26] This, like all aspects of dialectical thought, is relative to particular persons and situations. Thus one's totalization of his/her experience is detotalized and then retotalized by another person's experience.[27]

As an example, take a person who enters a room full of people who are in the midst of a conversation. Her/his totalization of the situation might be, "I am an interloper in this situation in which everyone is already engaged together in conversation. I feel un-

[24] Ibid., p. 43.
[25] Ibid., pp. 101–103.
[26] Ibid., p. 104.
[27] Ibid., p. 109.

easy." The person may act in such a way as to avoid the people in order to protect his/her autonomy, which may be threatened by the others. Now, one of the people already in the room may feel, "Oh, here is so-and-so. I've been waiting for him to come because he knows something about this matter which I want to hear. But he is aloof; maybe he feels haughty and doesn't wish to participate with those of us who know less than he does." Thus the interpersonal dynamic is cloudy, since no one knows where the other is; and the totalized view of the first person leads another to assume something different. In more psychological terms, we will find such analysis useful for examining communications among people so that we may discover the true nature of a given situation.

Cooper and Laing discuss theoretical aspects of human relations which can be illuminated by such a method. *Alteration* is one: it occurs when one's action passes from being-for-self to being-for-others. Given the alienated social relations of capitalism, alteration is a "necessary" transformation of communication, regardless of intent.[28] This might almost be called a misunderstanding based on the impossibility of real understanding. When alteration is applied to the creation of material goods by human labor, *objectification* occurs: "By the theft of his praxis through matter and the praxis of others, man's destiny becomes mechanical fatality, caught in the hell of the revolving field of practical passivity."[29]

Seriality follows alteration and objectification. It is the situation in which the group defines the context of action and thus in which any member of the group is interchangeable with any other. It is descriptive of the

28 Ibid., p. 118.
29 Ibid., pp. 117, 121–123.

thought and action which social class confers on members of the class; it is therefore a point in human relations at which autonomy and independence are totally in jeopardy. *Praxis* (self-action in a *project*) is the struggle against *process* (passive reception of action). It is the struggle against the alienation that creates actual powerlessness. Through it, the goal of the Sartrean method is revolutionary activity to end alienated society.[30]

For Laing and Cooper, presenting such a methodology was easier than putting it into practice. Antipsychiatry did not directly grow out of a political movement, much less a working-class movement. Therefore Laing and Cooper could not translate Sartre's method into class terms. Since they could not do that, they were unable to grasp the economic role of the nuclear family and/or the economic bases of sex-role development. Nor did they understand the changes in consciousness resulting from new forms of interpersonal relationships within the political movement (especially as transformed in the United States by the feminist movement). Laing and Cooper were not involved in active struggle and didn't have collective support. Nevertheless, that does not minimize their contribution. At the same period of time that they were writing, mass upsurges on the campuses of the United States were essentially moralistic and lacked the identical understanding that antipsychiatry lacked. While preparing the groundwork for future revolutionary activity, the majority of the New Left still did not totally understand what it was doing. It is the practical and theoretical work built upon that upsurge which has clarified the meaning of the upsurge. Similarly with antipsychiatry—*Reason and Violence*

[30] Ibid., pp. 123, 133.

began to explain Liang's earlier work and prepare him for *The Politics of Experience*.

FAMILIES AND BEYOND

The Politics of Experience, published in 1967, evidenced a major transformation in Laing's work. For the first time, Laing wrote publicly about his perceptions of the relationships between psychology and politics, concentrating on the repressive forces in Western culture and society, and showing the influence of politics on psychology. Being-for-others, fantasy as a mode of legitimate experience, the negation of experience by others—all returned from earlier work, although in much less abstract terms. The connections seemed clearer, even if made in a sagelike manner.

Family repression of children became the primary focus: "Long before a thermonuclear war can come about, we have had to lay waste our own sanity. We begin with the children. It is imperative to catch them in time. Without the most thorough and rapid brainwashing their dirty minds would see through our dirty tricks. Children are not yet fools, but we shall turn them into imbeciles like ourselves, with high IQs if possible."[31] And quoting Sartre:

> In fact, the world still seems to be inhabited by savages stupid enough to see reincarnated ancestors in their newborn children. Weapons and jewelry belonging to the dead men are waved under the infant's nose; if he makes a movement, there is a great shout—Grandfather has come back to life. This "old man" will suckle, dirty his straw, and bear the ancestral name; survivors

[31] R. D. Laing, *The Politics of Experience* (New York: Pantheon, 1967), p. 58.

of his ancient generation will enjoy seeing their comrade of hunts and battles wave his tiny limbs and bawl; as soon as he can speak they will inculcate recollections of the deceased. A severe training will "restore" his former character, they will remind him that "he" was wrathful, cruel, or magnanimous, and he will be convinced of it despite all evidence to the contrary. What barbarism! Take a living child, sew him up in a dead man's skin, and he will stifle in such senile childhood with no occupation save to reproduce the avuncular gestures, with no hope save to poison future childhoods after his own death. No wonder, after that, if he speaks of himself with the greatest precautions, half under his breath, often in the third person; this miserable creature is well aware that he is his own grandfather.

These backward aborigines can be found in the Fiji Islands, in Tahiti, in New Guinea, in Vienna, in Paris, in Rome, in New York—wherever there are men. They are called parents. Long before our birth, even before we are conceived, our parents have decided who we will be.[32]

Certainly this familial repression occurs in many societies, but to call it a part of all societies in the absence of class analysis is faulty. Laing, in his own poetic style, has chosen Sartre's poetic style to explain sweeping conceptualizations that would be much more helpful if they were further clarified. We are left, unfortunately, with a structure of repression without the hows and whys of that repression.

Laing does speak briefly of the coercive nature of the "nexal" family: "The 'protection' that such a family offers its members seems to be based on several preconditions: 1) a fantasy of the external world as extraordinarily dangerous; 2) the generation of terror inside the nexus at this external danger. The 'work' of

[32] Jean-Paul Sartre, Foreword to André Gorz, *The Traitor* quoted in Laing, *Politics of Experience* (New York: Pantheon, 1967), pp. 66–67.

the nexus is the generation of this terror. This work is *violence.*"[33] But Laing doesn't go beyond these perceptions to examine the actual day-to-day operations, the power, and the actual violence. These questions are left unanswered, although Laing was aware of the necessity of an expanded view:

> Questions and answers so far have been focused on the family as a social subsystem. Socially this work must now move to further understanding, not only of the internal disturbed and disturbing patterns of communications within families, of the double-binding procedures, the pseudo-mutuality, of what I have called the mystifications and the untenable positions, but also to the meaning of all this within the larger context of the civic order of society—that is, of the political order, of the ways people exercise control and power over one another.[34]

This expanded view shows understanding of the political order but not its origins. Laing no longer equivocates, however, on the possible validity of psychiatric mystification: *"Without exception* the experience and behavior that gets labeled schizophrenic is *a special strategy that a person invents in order to live in an unliveable situation."*[35] This, of course, was the general trend of Laing and Esterson in Sanity, *Madness and the Family,* but here it becomes much more politicized. The politicization occurs when Laing clearly sees the unlivable nature of capitalist social relations. Although he doesn't understand the class operations, he has a large sense of the overall cultural manifestations of capitalism. This is conveyed mainly as an understanding of the total mystification of reality by social institutions. It is a mystification so

33 Laing, *Politics of Experience,* p. 88.
34 Ibid., p. 123.
35 Ibid., p. 115.

complex, yet often so subtle, that there seems no escape—thus comes "schizophrenia" as a means of survival.

This line of reasoning brings Laing to the "schizophrenic voyage," with which he feels certain people can sort out their problems and be "reborn." The voyage is a journey, an "initiation ceremony," in which a person is propelled by the family or other social forces. During its course, the "ontological foundations are shaken," the world is called into question, the ego-boundaries are dissolved:

> True sanity entails in one way or another the dissolution of the normal ego, that false self competently adjusted to our alienated social reality; the emergence of the "inner" archetypal mediators of divine power, and through this death a rebirth, and the eventual re-establishment of a new kind of ego-functioning, the ego now being the servant of the divine, no longer its betrayer.[36]

Although Laing is well aware of the suffering undergone by those labeled schizophrenic, he sees the voyage as having aspects of romanticization of that suffering. Laing wonders why so many people who embark on the voyage don't remember.[37] This wonderment comes about because Laing is not clear about why the society will not tolerate people taking such trips. Such trips are caused by the alienation and oppression in the society, and attempts to fight that alienation and oppression are threatening to the social order. Since Laing fails to understand fully the contradictions in the schizophrenic journey, he usually fails to see other alternatives for helping people with their problems. The "breakdown" will not usually be a

---

[36] Ibid., pp. 118, 132–133, 144–145.
[37] Ibid., p. 118.

"breakthrough" for most people; most of them will wind up in the back wards of mental prisons.

Laing's inability to synthesize the material-political elements with the spiritual is unfortunate. Some reasons for this are, as mentioned earlier, lack of political involvement and collective support. Laing's tremendous jump forward in understanding so much of what happens with people's minds was so monumental that the lack of context and collective support created a dead end. He knew too much and had no place to put that knowledge into practice. Also, so many of Laing's adherents kept his ideas in an apolitical framework. As a result, Laing's work became stagnant and he wrote less and less about political struggle.

David Cooper, meanwhile, began to take up the political basis of antipsychiatry. His *Psychiatry and Anti-Psychiatry*[38] appeared the same year as Laing's *Politics of Experience*. The two books are quite similar in their critique of mainstream psychology and psychiatry, although Cooper doesn't approach the spiritual realm, as does Laing. *Anti-Psychiatry* is less idealistic, focusing on the day-to-day matters of psychological work.

Cooper includes a section on his work at Villa 21, an experimental ward of a mental hospital in which radical methods of therapy and deprofessionalization were tried and where patients to some extent acted as therapists for each other. This appeared to Cooper as the most radical departure from traditional psychiatry, and he realized some of the contradictions in such a plan:

[38] David Cooper, *Psychiatry and Anti-Psychiatry* (New York: Ballantine, 1967).

> A certain basic materiality in the situation remains. Staff are paid to be there, patients are not. Staff are paid according to their official role and rank.[39]

> The "experiment" of the unit has had one quite certain "result" and one certain "conclusion." The result is the establishment of the limits of institutional change, and these limits are found to be very closely drawn indeed—even in a progressive mental hospital.[40]

Cooper, however, was yet to realize the revolutionary implications of this situation. While understanding that capitalism was the cause and that the disciplinary nature of psychiatry was succeeding in resuscitating capitalism, Cooper was unsure of what transformation was needed. Patients needed to be integrated into the "community," but what did that mean for Cooper? Would the community that had labeled them now reaccept them? Cooper, like Laing, was restricted by the contradictions between psychological and political practice.

Laing's next book, *The Politics of the Family,*[41] was the beginning of the retreat of antipsychiatry. Remaining with a structural approach to families, Laing wondered what method would tell us more about family operations: "Families (of some kind or other, albeit *very* different from ours) have existed, say, for at least 100,000 years. We can study directly only a minute slice of the family chain: three generations, if we are lucky. Even studies of three generations are rare. What patterns can we hope to find, when we are restricted to three out of at least 4000

[39] David Cooper, *The Death of the Family* (New York: Pantheon, 1970), pp. 116–117.

[40] Ibid., p. 121.

[41] R. D. Laing, *The Politics of the Family* (New York: Pantheon, 1969).

generations?"[42] This is a false barrier. Families have so changed over those one hundred thousand years that any resemblances are minimal. Particularly when the development of class society is kept in mind, the family of one hundred thousand years ago becomes a grouping of people based neither on surplus value nor on the division of labor. The required method for studying—and changing—family operations is one that analyzes the class, power, and social arrangements of today's bourgeois nuclear family. The production of wealth and the reproduction of class society by the family tell more about oppression and alienation than do archetypes of family groupings in antiquity or prehistory. Without such an analytical method, Laing and antipsychiatry could not continue even to ask the right questions, much less to answer them.

Given the shortcomings of antipsychiatry, what were its chances for developing in a different sense, for finally grasping the Marxism with which it had flirted at earlier points? Laing's *Knots*[43] certainly wasn't about to do this. *Knots* is essentially a series of poetic vignettes dealing with collusion and the double-bind in family and social situations. The numerous individual pieces, becoming more "complicated" throughout the book, are actually little more than applied exercises in communications theory. They remain as independent structures, without motion in any dialectical sense.

As an example:

My mother loves me.
    I feel good.
I feel good because she loves me.

[42] Ibid., p. 20.
[43] R. D. Laing, *Knots* (New York: Pantheon, 1970).

> I am good because I feel good
> I feel good because I am good
> My mother loves me because I am good.
>
> My mother does not love me.
>   I feel bad.
> I feel bad because she does not love me
>   I am bad because I feel bad
> I feel bad because I am bad
> I am bad because she does not love me
> She does not love me because I am bad.[44]

Take the sequence (1) Mother doesn't love me, (2) I feel bad, and (3) I am bad; or its converse, (1) I am bad, (2) I feel bad, and (3) Mother doesn't love me. Are these logical "therefore," or are they part of a dialectic? We would place them in a dialectical sequence of defined behavior in which entire life situations were involved. We would want to know more about these sequential acts and feelings. Maybe in the first sequence feeling bad (2) doesn't always follow the lack of Mother's love (1); maybe being bad (3) doesn't always follow feeling bad (2). Maybe the converse is always coexistent (but not in the necessary order). Maybe all operations coexist, in different and changing ways.

Now of course, we realize that Laing has presented us with vignettes, not case histories or Marxist analyses of family situations. Nevertheless, it seems mystifying to place these sequences on paper as they are, since all we can end up with are simplified (and even reified) applications of communications theory to people's oppressed existence. True, the pieces in *Knots* can be seen as tight capsule versions of doublebinds and other mystified experience, but to justify the existence of a book full of these capsules calls for

[44] Ibid., p. 9.

the acceptance of two assumptions. First, there is the assumption that the reader fully understands the previous works of Laing and the other antipsychiatrists. Second, there is the assumption that these vignettes are useful, even to the reader who comprehends the backdrop of ten years of antipsychiatry.

The disappointing part is that Laing's logical vignettes could have been translated into more meaningful descriptions of the oppressive interpersonal relationships in society. Lacking a dialectical-materialist method, Laing could not make the much-needed translation. At the same time as Laing failed, Aaron Esterson attempted this difficult task.

Esterson has gone further than any of the other antipsychiatrists in exploring the *detailed operations* of the family, as well as the social context of these operations. In *The Leaves of Spring*[45] he has done two things: first, he has taken the family of Sarah Danzig (from his and Laing's *Sanity, Madness and the Family*) and greatly expanded our knowledge of it, explaining nearly all of the behavior of the family members in light of real circumstances; second, he has written about the theory and methodology of dialectical materialism as applied to psychology.

Esterson shows how *all* of Sarah's fears were fears of real things, not "paranoid" fears as the professionals and the family thought. In detail he demonstrates how the ward nurses kept messages from her, how her parents lied about supposed visits, how her family was conspiratorial. When Sarah was not present at the interviews, the conspiratorial nature of the family gave the family members "a solidarity otherwise lacking. It is impressive how their conflicts are

[45] Aaron Esterson, *The Leaves of Spring* (London: Tavistock, 1971).

then forgotten."[46] Sarah's "madness" was seen as a "calamity" visited upon the family, a calamity that threatened to break their "united family front." We learn, of course, that the unity was a very superficial front: throughout the family's history, there were always changing alliances among members.[47] The Danzigs were serving two masters, God and public opinion. These masters held the family together as a serial group; when Sarah threatened the continued serving of these masters, she became the "external object" of seriality in a family whose total being was being-for-others.[48]

Esterson presents the many material forces involved in the creation of this serial group and its accompanying operations: included are the father's business relations, his orthodox religion, Mr. and Mrs. Danzig's marriage of convenience and subsequent unsatisfactory sexual relations, and different social conditions from those of the "old country" (Eastern Europe) from which Mr. and Mrs. Danzig's parents had come.[49] In each case the materiality comes through. For instance, Mr. Danzig saw children as an investment, a attitude that Esterson relates to his own businesslike marriage and his daily business relations.[50]

Another example is Sarah's intensive reading of the Bible. Taught by her father the importance of knowing the Bible, Sarah began to fulfill that task. As she read it more, her parents saw her getting "sicker." At first the Danzigs saw this as compulsion, whereas

[46] Ibid., p. 9.
[47] Ibid., pp. 12, 17.
[48] Ibid., pp. 37–38, 53, 58.
[49] Ibid., pp. 40, 48, 131–132, 145.
[50] Ibid., pp. 46–48.

in reality Sarah was responding with the fact that women simply weren't allowed to educate themselves in Judaism. When Sarah found this out, she began to understand that religion, like everything else in her family, was governed by a double standard.[51]

Sarah's new-found understanding became a danger to the family structure. Unlike her brother, John, she refused to "come of age" by giving up "thinking for herself," a feature that her parents always saw as a symptom of illness. As Mrs. Danzig put it: "Sitting up all night thinking and not telling anyone what she thought. Not that we particularly want to know what Sarah's thinking or doing, although it's only natural that a mother should be curious.[52]

The parents were not invading Sarah's privacy out of innocent curiosity—they had real fears that Sarah was "ill" and felt that they could "help" her. Mr. Danzig's disciplinary methods, which he likened to those of the police and army,[53] were intended to enforce "correct" behavior ("I'm only interfering when I see something which I don't like").[54] The more the family was threatened by Sarah's attempt at independence, the more they cracked down. Behavior that they used to call "lazy" was now called "doing nothing"—and what good was a person if she were not engaged in "socially correct" work?

It is important that Esterson not only provides real reasons for Sarah's behavior, but also provides reasons for the other family members' behavior. One area, however, in which he slips up is in explaining away Mr. Danzig's behavior by psychoanalytic con-

51 Ibid., pp. 24–25, 138–139, 200–201.
52 Ibid., p. 23.
53 Ibid., p. 40.
54 Ibid., p. 104.

structs. A number of times we are treated to interpretations such as the loose domestic arrangements being a reflection of loose bowel control or Mr. Danzig's transgressions of the Sabbath (lighting a match and smoking a cigarette) being anal masturbatory components of his disobedience.[55] It is disappointing that Esterson has not transcended such downright vulgar Freudianism; but more important, there is a real blocking up of Esterson's possibilities, caused by his failure to make a total break with traditional frameworks. For instance, he *imputes* much less intelligible behavior and awareness to Sarah than his descriptions have *shown:* "The more they mystified her the more she remained naïve, and the more she remained naïve the more they felt they had to protect themselves by mystifying her."[56] Quite the contrary! Sarah was not naïve; the family was threatened because Sarah had *caught on.* In fact, Esterson has not totally given up the pathology model. After condemning psychiatric positivism, he states: "This is not an argument, of course, against recognizing that some people are mad. It is an argument for recognizing who the mad ones are, and an argument against the assumption that psychiatric training fits psychiatrists to do the recognizing."[57] Although Esterson admits that psychiatrists are "bad" labelers, he obviously believes that there can be "good" labelers.

What is really unfortunate about these regressions to psychoanalytic theory is that Esterson is aware of the dialectical method—in fact, he claims to have used it throughout the entire book. In the second part of the book he discusses his interpretation of dialecti-

[55] Ibid., p. 12.
[56] Ibid., p. 226.
[57] Ibid., p. 266.

cal method in quite a rigorous manner.[58] He is convincing enough without drumming up some nonsensical Freudian myths to cloud the dialectics. It seems clear that Esterson was able to give the most detailed antipsychiatric description of the family due to awareness of dialectical method, as well as a basically materialist perspective. From one who achieved this clarity of description, the relative lack of further analysis is disappointing.

David Cooper's *Death of the Family* is less dialectical in theory than Esterson's *Leaves* but proffers a more political strategy. Yet the partial nature of Cooper's approach results in his political strategy being quite adventurist. He sees the family as tied by a false bond that must be smashed, but he fails to understand the contradictions of the family being simultaneously the basic oppressive socializing institution and the basic emotional support network for most people. Concentrating on the plasticity of the present-day nuclear family, Cooper overlooks its economic role in society.

The twentieth-century family not only reproduces human labor but also serves as a major unit of consumption. Capitalism survives in part by producing and selling more than what is needed—for instance, communal living requires fewer appliances, less rent, less human labor, etc. Further, in the secluded circle of the nuclear family, false answers to real needs are created. One example of this is the selling of nonessential commodities for the house and family by using techniques of sexual enticement. Yet for all this materialism, bourgeois psychology tells people that they shouldn't be so materialistic. The result is a

[58] Esterson's interpretation is essentially based on Laing and Cooper's *Reason and Violence*.

mystification of how the process works, and people are taught to blame themselves rather than the system.

At times Cooper understands the complexity of contradictions within the family, yet his lack of class analysis and his metaphorical descriptions often obscure the possibilities of going further. He deals with the institutionalized concept of love in relation to the family. We must view love as a concept that has been fantasized due to its usefulness in covering up real (political) family conflicts. But Cooper doesn't point this out before going into his many loose definitions of love, definitions involving such vague terms as "mutual respect," "trust," and "freedom to love." With these terms, Cooper goes on to say that this "real" love is seen as "subversive," especially in terms of the nuclear family:

> The appearance of love is subversive to any good social ordering of our lives. Far more than being statistically abnormal, love is dangerous, it might even spread through the aseptic shield that we get each other to erect around ourselves. What we are socially conditioned to need and expect is not love, but security. Security means the full and repeatedly reinforced affirmation of the family.[59]

It is true that security means the affirmation of the family. The life style created by capitalist family structure results in people having no other basis of security. On the other hand, attempts at real security and nonalienated love are threatening to the society and are prevented by the family's daily operations:

> The family, over the last two centuries, has mediated an evasiveness into the lives of individuals that is essential to the continued operation of imperializing capitalism. The family, definitionally, can never leave

[59] Cooper, *Death of the Family*, p. 39.

> one alone, as it is the hypostatization of the ultimately perfected mass medium. The family is the television box replete with color, touch, taste, and smell effects that has been taught to forget how to turn off.[60]

The family, however, doesn't do this simply to bother its members, but rather to enforce the socialization process.

As monopoly capitalism approaches the crisis situation that may lead it into fascism, the functions of the family become more dangerous:

> The emotional sense of fascism, at this point in time, is terrifyingly extended. It is no longer simply a matter of militia and police in the interests of monopoly capitalism in crisis. The most benevolent institutions of our society become our oppressors, in a way that relegates the gas chambers of Auschwitz to the level of a naïve, fumbling attempt at massacre; the last expiring, cyanimized breath is only the beginning of torture.[61]

But this overlooks the class structure of society and the various roles played by families of different classes. Whereas for Cooper "the blood of consanguinity has already flowed down the gutters of suburban family streets,"[62] for most people living under capitalism the blood has also flowed between classes and between black and white. That is, the family, in a reified view, can become the focus of much angry energy at the expense of being located within the complete social order. Lacking such a method, Cooper is left without a coherent political program within which to rebuild the way people live. Although he demands a self-confrontation of love-struggle and the creation of a sexuality (including homosexuality)

60 Ibid., p. 140.
61 Ibid., p. 93.
62 Ibid., p. 141.

that would be "an open possibility, never a duty,"[63] Cooper remains an individualistic and idealistic revolutionary. He seeks a revolution of Molotov cocktails and sexual liberation, but his praise of Mao, Che, and urban guerrilla warfare reflects the same limited view that the New Left often indulged in. Such a conception of revolution is "tailist" in that it follows on the tails of other revolutionary movements rather than building a movement based on the conditions of modern Western capitalism.

This limited view of revolution is reinforced by Cooper's style of writing (much like Laing's), a style in which the poetic nuances seem more self-gratifying than critical. It is as if a pundit were giving out the truth, adding poetic asides to decorate the often bare skeleton of real praxis.

Cooper wants to destroy the family (good; the family is oppressive and must be destroyed), but is this possible in a single stroke, is this possible without a socialist revolution as a precondition? Can all the working-class women and children now being supported by men simply *give up* the family and call the giving up a revolutionary act? It should be clear to any serious political activist that capitalist economic realities prevent the total breakdown of the nuclear family except in such a way that men would get the greatest benefit, given their position in society.

Even in this most radical critique of the family we never get an understanding of why this mutilating, butchering, murdering, alienating institution has not just been consigned to the dung heap of history. We are never given a sufficient sense of the social weight of the family as connected to the objective necessities of capitalist society. By implication we are led to

[63] Ibid., p. 46.

believe that the people who live and endure these sufferings do so because they are fools. Further, the social conditions have not yet reached a political level (via organization) at which such a total rupture with tradition would be possible. To pose the death of the family to the average household in this country would be no more than a scare tactic, resulting in their alienation from the socialist movement. *Death of the Family* speaks mainly to those privileged enough to do without the family—in other words, the free-floating street revolutionaries imagined by Cooper.

Morton Schatzman's *Soul Murder*[64] *is the newest* addition to antipsychiatry and quite a novel book in its area. Schatzman examines the "mental illness" of Daniel Paul Schreber, whose *Memoirs* are considered a classic, and contrasts the *Memoirs* with the work of Schreber's father, Daniel Gottlieb Moritz Schreber. The elder Schreber, a noted physician and authority on child-rearing, was a prominent influence in mid- to late-nineteenth-century German society.

We are shown how all the "symptoms" of young Schreber's "illness" are directly attributable to his father's authoritarian theory and practice of child-rearing. The son almost paraphrases the father when he speaks of guilt over masturbation, fear of outside forces, feelings of persecution and restraint. Dr. Schreber used his remarkable inventions on his son: they included devices to restrain the child on his back in bed, and to prevent masturbation, contraptions to develop good posture by keeping the chin pushed up straight from the body, and other similar gadgets.

In the elder Schreber's widely read books are advocated rigid schedules of exercise, forced winter swim-

---

[64] Morton Schatzman, *Soul Murder* (New York: Pantheon, 1973).

ming, arbitrary parental authority, and many aspects of authoritarian middle-class life which were then generally accepted. Schatzman quotes father and son, one after the other, to show us how the authoritarian conditioning was bound to drive the son mad. We see how the prescriptions of the father led to the son's "hallucinations" and perception of "miracles." For instance, the father's prohibitions against comfortable posture led to the son's "coccyx miracle": "an extremely painful, caries-like state of the lower vertebrae. Its purpose was *to make sitting and even lying down impossible*." A device to force rigid posture by pushing up on the chest led to the "compression-of-the-chest-miracle."[65] At times Daniel Paul was aware of something going on other than internalized symptoms: " 'At the time when my nervous illness seemed almost incurable, I gained the conviction that soul murder had been attempted on me by somebody. . . .' " Still the son could not connect the soul murder to his father.

Schatzman is able to show that connection. The young Schreber is a classic example of the direct translation of oppression into "mental illness." Further, the aspects of that translation are clear: They revolve around the bourgeois ethic promoted by the elder Schreber and around the Victorian world in which that ethic existed. Seen as an individual, Daniel Paul appears to be utterly crazy; seen as a product of his father's severe control, the son appears to be a victim. Family authority today may have become more rational and less overtly repressive, but the basic content remains: society is reproduced by the family, with those who fail to conform winding up categorized as mentally ill. Unfortunately, Schatzman doesn't

[65] Ibid., pp. 43, 46.

bring the process up to date, leaving us only with a brief look into the history of family repression. But by building on such partial methods as those offered by Schatzman and other antipsychiatrists, it is possible to approach the overall method needed to understand the modern family's support of the status quo.

Antipsychiatry has provided a major advance in understanding the political operations that have been called psychological. With its ability to incorporate so much of family problems, antipsychiatry has enabled many people to attack the so-called scientific foundations of psychiatry and psychology. Combined with the more Marxist analyses of Reich and Fanon, antipsychiatry was a major break with traditional psychology and psychiatry, and it is the revolutionary kernel within antipsychiatry on which we must build a Marxist psychology.

7. Beyond Therapy

THE THERAPIST–PATIENT RELATIONSHIP

As such a large part of this book deals with critiques of therapy, what then will replace therapy? The first thing to understand is that "therapy" has many different meanings. The clearest definition is "the use of power to control behavior." What is today considered therapy was once the province of the clergy (inquisitor or father confessor) and the family.

The therapist deals with behavior problems that present an obnoxious face to the public, with personal feelings that exemplify antisocial attitudes, and with people's needs for companionship. It is obvious that this is the role of the nonhospital therapist—psychiatric hospitalization is a police function dealt with earlier. The therapist-patient relationship is aggressive-passive, leader-led, dominant-submissive, and any other number of polarities. The therapist is set up as an expert in dealing with human problems, much like the computer technician is set up as an expert in the electronics of computers. Reflecting our technocratic social attitudes, the therapist deals in skills and techniques rather than in understanding and feeling.

While the patient (nonactive person) pours out her troubles, the therapist remains aloof from any honest communication. His ethic prevents personal contact of any sort.[1] Therapists rarely understand the class, social, and phenomenological worlds of their clients—they have little knowledge of the client's background and little experience in the client's world view.

The therapist performs a function that could and should be carried out by friends: that of helping people solve their problems. But we have been desensitized and fragmented to the extent that we do not trust those who know us with our "secrets." In place of friendship the therapist-patient relationship occurs. Picture the common conversation of someone in therapy who has lost the ability to define him/herself except through the therapist: "I was going to go away for the weekend, but my therapist says it would be escaping." Or that of the person whose problems are now purged from him/her via the therapist's exorcism: "That's something I've been dealing with in therapy. My therapist knows what's going on." How many people run around saying, "my therapist" this, "my therapist" that, losing track of their own place in the situation?

[1] Some readers may question this in terms of the "humanistic" school or "third camp" therapies. Psychodrama, gestalt therapy, bio-energetics, encounter groups, sensitivity training, etc., appear to have much contact, but in reality that contact is a further mystification and alienation, since it is still forced and contrived rather than integral to the relationship. Touching, body movement, and the like, are techniques and exercises, not spontaneous gestures. Even when they sometimes really are spontaneous, they are still isolated from the rest of the therapeutic contact.

At such a point, the relationship is *reified* (objectified, turned into an abstract structure rather than a dynamic and moving action). Like most social relating in our society, this reification occurs at the expense of the least powerful—in this case, the patient. To discover this is to leave therapy, itself often a difficult action, given the built-up dependencies. And the therapist is safe in his office, saying, "You're not leaving me, you're leaving your problems." Since most of our "problems" are defined as such by the therapy industry rather than by our own realities, perhaps it is good to leave them.

WHAT ARE PROBLEMS?

Most problems with which people approach therapists are obvious social facts that have been internalized. In other words, the problems are real events in our society; years of education and media exposure have made us feel that these problems are specific to us. For instance, masturbation fears are a problem caused by school, religion, and parents, but the fears are intensely taken in by the person, who feels it is *his* problem.

As I mentioned in the chapter on Reich, internalization is a major problem of our psychic structure. It has altered us from active persons to passive recipients of the "inevitable" or the "correct." How scared people are of speaking out loud those daily thoughts and feelings that seem so personal but are really mass acculturation! We can look to the impact of the women's movement on therapy: many women realized that it was not a singularly personal matter to be depressed as a housewife or frustrated over lack of sexual satisfaction, so clearly therapy was not about to provide the answers that a consciousness-raising group could. What if we took this as a definitive move in social liberation and applied it on a large scale?

Most of the specific problems dealt with in therapy concern sexuality, sex roles, and physiological aspects of sexual functioning. People are scared of sexual relations or of seeking unabandoned pleasure in them. Social and interpersonal pressures cause these people to keep quiet and work the problems out by any of several repressive methods: abstinence, retreat into the family, sublimation, or therapy (which may demand all of the preceding). Contraception and abortion cause terrible guilt feelings and self-recrimination, since most people are kept from adequate and safe methods. Sex roles determine such a large part of our behavior that it is unlikely to find more than a small minority of problems not related to them. We have been conditioned to a double standard for everything to the point where we are usually unaware of the most intricate subtleties involving "male" or "female" character. Homosexuality, and much heterosexuality, fit into the category of "deviant" or "maladjusted" behavior, and it becomes almost impossible to engage in free expression of sexuality unless we have successfully internalized what we've learned.

Alienation from work also constitutes a large percentage of people's problems. How can people be happy and fulfilled when they sell their labor, performing alienated and oppressive work that tends to be split totally from other aspects of their lives? Assembly lines, hospital laundries, business offices, and sales counters do not exactly fulfill *human* needs, although there is no doubt that they fulfill *economic* needs. Even people engaged in artistic or creative jobs (certainly a category difficult to define) wind up selling their creativity for financial considerations. For a working class to build a nation and then be denied a part in the wealth they have produced is certainly a cause of problems. Internalization of these problems has taken deep root; however, we see the problems but not the solutions. To be aware and sensitive today means to face the possibilities of madness and/or revolution.[2] Given this choice, the ruling class seems to have succeeded for the time being, since more people are going mad than going revolutionary.

Other practical problems present themselves in the therapy situation. People need to leave their parents, to live in a supportive environment, and to find a peer group. They have been convinced that their failings are the cause of these problems, so they come for therapy. *Therapists will not provide the obvious answers, since that will put them out of business.*

WHAT CAN WE DO?

Given that the problems are obvious, let's deal with them. When a person comes to you with a problem, treat her/him as a human being, and don't feel that you can't be of help—this goes for therapists and non-therapists. Work out problems with your own insights and needs—you may have the same problem. We need to get people together for consciousness-raising/ rap groups in which they can discuss, as equals, real problems. We need to find supportive groups that will help with communal living arrangements and alternative jobs, groups for people working in straight jobs which will help them organize for economic and per-

[2] This last sentence is prompted by an article by Russell Jacoby, "The Politics of Subjectivity," in *Telos,* 9 (Fall 1971): 118.

sonal needs on the job, groups of people sharing the same oppression—like women, gays, children, blacks, etc.

We have to realize that we can get collective strength from collective effort, that a detached professional is not always needed. This is not to say that such a method will not be available to people seeking help, but instead of seeing therapy as the only answer for them, we must begin to construct self-help groups that will reach beyond student-freak-intellectual constituencies.

This all sounds simplistic to many people who are convinced that such approaches cannot be set up. I don't suggest for a moment that it is easy, but I do maintain that it is necessary and possible. I have spoken to many people who have had the need for self-help groups or just for validation that they weren't crazy. And such needs are beginning to be met by the people's own efforts. There is much arrogance in the attitudes of many therapists (and others), who feel that people won't respond to such methods. Why, then, are so many self-help groups in existence? Why have people set up consciousness-raising groups, child-care centers, work groups, and so on, if they are not aware of the collective problems?

A Marxist movement interested in a better society cannot ignore the needs that manifest themselves so strongly. Local organizations based on Reich's Sex-Pol organization would be of immense importance in showing youth the relation of political and sexual repression and in providing them with their own private places where they could make love without fear. Networks of feminist and gay counselors already exist, and the expansion of such groups would provide help to many people. Work groups, organizing workshops, food co-ops, independent child-care facilities, all combine to offer alternatives to many of the daily problems of capitalist America. Yet many organizers do not see this function. They have not yet realized the immense problem-solving possibilities of the integration of political and cultural revolution. Particularly in the mental health fields, many professionals and paraprofessionals detach their political selves from their work, not realizing the power they have to change the ideological conditions of oppression, as well as the economic conditions.

"Radical therapists," living in a contradiction of self-definition, need to learn new ways—they need to explore the possibilities of relating to people as active human beings, not as passive people with problems. They need to stop approaching people as "troubled" and to begin approaching them as oppressed. Radicals are supposed to approach everything radically, so why do they exclude the therapy industry from their radicalism? It is hard to give up professional privileges, but the times are demanding that more and more. The smooth liberalism of the shrinking business is quickly eroding, and the trend to collective support is growing.

THE MENTAL PATIENTS' LIBERATION MOVEMENT

In the United States and other countries mental patients' liberation fronts are growing. Most people have not heard of these organizations, but they are becoming increasingly important. Most of the groups are composed of ex-patients, although some have existed inside state hospitals. These groups function on many levels: as consciousness-raisers/problem-solvers, as political action groups to secure patients' rights and release of patients, and as alternatives to traditional mental health models.[3]

Working in the *Rough Times* collective, I had much contact with most of the mental patients' liberation groups, and I have learned much from them, including ways of carrying on my own political work in a more complete way. The patients' groups are not all in agreement on all the issues involved, but they share a political and personal opposition to the system that has attempted to do them in. From first fighting against lobotomies and involuntary commitment, patients' groups are finding more and more failings in bourgeois America and are beginning to get involved in other political struggles as well. Like the women's and gay movements, the mental patients' movement is attacking deep-seated and traditional authority and ideology. The issues involved—on the simplest level psychiatric atrocities, on the widest level the destruction of human freedom by capitalism—are important to all concerned with a total revolutionary transformation.

In Vancouver, British Columbia, the Mental Patients Association has hundreds of members. It has set up a drop-in center, two "therapeutic communities" run by the residents, and a farm that attempts to produce much of the food consumed by members and also provides a good place to get away to. I had a remarkable visit there in November 1972, exchanging ideas, tactics, and feelings with many M.P.A. people. The atmosphere of the drop-in center, where I spent most of my time, was a combination of politics, emotional support, comradeship, and personal growth—a

[3] *Rough Times*, vol. 3, no. 2 (October–November 1972), is devoted to mental patients' rights and organizing. It contains statements by, and information on, many groups.

kind of political model for persons wishing to integrate the divergent aspects of their lives, a process in which we are all hopefully engaged.

In addition to being involved in M.P.A. and related activities, many of the members were active in other political spheres. This has also been the case with many people in other patients' groups—the particular struggles of these groups has led them to create more revolutionary possibilities than just those centered around the antipsychiatry movement. It appears that getting one's head together in a supportive political environment has immense possibilities for energizing people to participate in the larger political struggle.

Mental patients' liberation groups in other cities have done similar things. Philadelphia Mental Patients Liberation Project (P.M.P.L.P.) organized a demonstration at a large psychosurgery conference. New York M.P.L.P. members have made many appearances in the media and on the streets. The activities are too many to name here.

In Heidelberg, West Germany, the Socialist Patients Collective (S.P.K.) has been a model of political struggle. The S.P.K. transformed itself from just a patients group to a major political organization, involving itself in many important areas. Government repression was swift, and some of the dozens of members arrested remain in jail after more than a year (at this writing). The S.P.K. began with a highly developed Marxist approach, joining with many other political forces and showing those others what the power of their movement was.

Revolutionary politics have emerged in many ways in the past. Mental patients' liberation and similar political expressions are growing as the contradictions within capitalism change their balance. As our society enters its final stages, the behavior and human existence labeled "mad" by those in power takes on new forms. What used to be madness is now revolution.

FEMINIST THERAPY

One of the political approaches to alternatives to the regular therapy routine is the spread of feminist therapy collectives around the country.[4] These groups have grown out of the feminist movement and seek to provide women with a form of help hitherto unavailable to them. Women seeking nonoppressive therapists are faced with a difficult situation because the majority of therapists are men who side with traditional male models of "mental health," telling women to adjust and be passive. The feminist therapy collectives offer sisterhood more than professionalism, seeking to bring to light the common problems of women which have been labeled as "mental illness," etc.

The political approach of feminism has led to a different outlook on what therapy should be. The women's therapy groups have begun to transform the so-called therapeutic into the realm of liberation. Their opposition to the strong values of "manhood" which are implicit and explicit in conventional therapy has been an important model for others seeking alternative modes of helping people. It is a clear case of determining the priorities—here they are that feminism is the guiding method of help and self-help.

In Somerville, Massachusetts, the Women's Therapy Collective works together with the Somerville Women's Health Project, a free clinic geared to the

[4] See "Feminist Psychology Coalition," *Rough Times*, vol. 3, no. 1 (September 1972).

needs of the women of this predominantly working-class city. The collective sees itself as tied to the larger struggle of women's liberation, although the focus of its work is meeting women's needs for help with personal problems. In New York City the Feminist Psychology Coalition comprises several projects, one of them a therapy referral service. Some of the people in the collective see women who call, but they have a larger referral network of women therapists who are in tune with the requisites of feminist help/self-help. These groups are attempting to break down many of the professionalist barriers to truly open self-help. Part of this has meant working with nonprofessionals to demystify therapy and to "train" community women as counselors.

BEYOND THERAPY

Without an adequate system of providing help and self-help to the many people seeking it, how can we talk of going beyond therapy? It should be clear that this does not disregard people's needs for therapists. Many people need to see an "outsider," since they don't have a good support group of their own. Given this, alternative therapy centers should be set up, but these counterinstitutions should keep two main things in mind: first, the large institutions of the mental health establishment cannot be forgotten—they require strong and militant organizing efforts for the patients and workers. Second, the goal of radical therapy, alternative therapy, etc., should be to put itself out of business. This means transformation and transcendence of the therapy model and the construction of new, humanistic, politically relevant ways for people to help one another. Revolutionary society is a clear goal, and in it we would have support groups where we work, where we live, where we play, everywhere. If we keep our vision of the future, we can better know the problems of the present struggle.

8. Toward Sexual Integration

SEXUALITY AND MARXIST PSYCHOLOGY

An understanding of sexuality is integral to the formulation of a theory of Marxist psychology. Previous chapters have shown where sexuality fits into the social structure. In the chapter on the medical model it was seen as a moral code enforced by the mental health professionals (and their predecessors). In the chapter on Freudianism it was demonstrated how the deep roots of sexuality were "uncovered" and used in the construction of the Freudian world view, based on sexual repression and sublimation. Reich teaches us that sexual repression and social repression are two aspects of the same thing. In the antipsychiatry chapter we saw how at various times women's sexual feelings were major factors in their oppression by the shrink-parent forces.

This recurrence of sexual factors is no accident—it is due to the incredible importance of sexuality in human existence. I have spoken of this in earlier chapters; here I wish to expand on the meaning of sexuality and on some specific elements. This is based primarily on a Reichian perspective, although I remain well aware of the limitations of that perspective. I have placed this chapter here so that the foregoing material would lead up to it; sexuality can now be discussed using terms and ideas already formulated. Also, as I will show in the final chapter, sexual liberation is an integral part of the coming revolution and should be understood in that light.

SEXUALITY IN SOCIETY

It seems pointless to engage in the common but diversionary argument about whether or not sexuality is the primary force in human existence. What is necessary is to realize its tremendous importance, to understand its impact on our lives, and to find ways of integrating sexual liberation with other aspects of human liberation.

There is no way to give a definition of sexuality that will be totally satisfactory, but definitions ought to be changeable anyway. Sexuality is an aspect of human existence that involves both sexual reproduction and pleasure, and the ways in which people relate to those. It includes thought, feeling, "vibrations," behavior, social restrictions, and interpersonal relationships involving sex. It further includes the social relations built up around itself. And at the integrative level sexuality involves the unity of all forms of human relationships as expressed in terms of sexual behavior; this can be seen as the integration of body, mind, and spirit. Sexuality does not imply, as defined here, solely genital sex; it involves that, as well as other touch and nontouch *communications* between people which bring forth or lead to integration as described above. What we sense in sexual encounters is pleasure, pain, hurt, warmth, honesty, oppression, etc.—in short, all the possible sensations and feelings that would apply to the rest of the world. But pleasure in sexuality is certainly more than momentary gratification or simple orgasm: it is pleasure that transcends the "ordinary" pleasures and sensations, what we might call a primal force that is (striving to be) at unity with our existence in the world. Given this lengthy definition, where does it lead?

In the Garden of Eden myth the serpent of knowledge leads the first humans to cover their genitals (not their noses or feet). In the drama of Jesus sex is denied as a factor in the Messiah's birth, since it would tarnish his role as the son of (an asexual) God. Throughout history, religion and myth have provided society with the justification to repress sexuality. While torturing "witches" accused of sexual deviations, inquisitors released some of their own sexual repression by stripping the women and shaving off all their body hair. Wherever we look, sex is the hidden, evil, corrupting secret—and people have been engaging in the secret act without letting themselves in on the secret.

Until recently nearly all doctors, clergymen, educators, and other influential professionals told people the "truth" of how masturbation leads to damnation and/or insanity. Swaddling and other restraints eventually became unnecessary, since people internalized the fears at an early age. Rape and war have always been corollaries. The Boston Lesbian Feminists write of how the act of war, particularly of soldiers, stems from the same male-dominated social structure as does the act of rape: they quote the oft-heard army training camp chant, "This is my rifle, this is my gun. One is for killing, one is for fun."[1]

Sexuality today has become an area of what Marcuse calls "repressive desublimation," in which aspects of existence previously channeled into other areas (sublimated) are now brought into the open (desublimated) in repressive ways. For instance, public talk of seduction used to be forbidden and was channeled into chivalry, manners, and so on; now seduction raps are used to sell products. The result of repressive desublimation is a modern authoritarian order that caters to the real needs of people but supplies false answers. The media and advertising preoccupation with sexuality operates along these lines, providing what might seem like a diversion to the increasing breakdown of capitalism. Sexuality in such a situation is totally linked to objects—their acquisition, use, destruction—and the human parts of sexuality are stripped away.

Of course, once a factor is brought to light, its contradictions begin to appear. Thus more information and activities in sexual areas of existence tend to provide for certain possibilities of turning sex around and using it for liberating purposes. Attaining a prominent position in daily life, sex begins to be demystified. The next step is to break through the confusion and mystification of that level and to advance to a liberating level. An example of the contradictions in this area is recent advances in contraception. These advances help women to enjoy their sexuality with men without fear of pregnancy—and

[1] Boston Lesbian Feminists, "Vietnam: A Feminist Analysis," *Rough Times* (New York: Ballantine, 1973), pp. 228–233.

for both women and men, it is important to have safety in order to explore new sexual areas. The contradictory side is that "safe sex" is misused by men who see women as "more available."

Reich and the Sex-Pol struggle pushed for free and easy contraceptives and youth centers where lovers could be alone. This type of struggle attracted many political (and nonpolitical) youths who desperately needed to save their life force in the midst of a repressive society. Whereas their movement was not sufficiently liberated to present the possibility of totally nonrepressed sexuality, the same social trend exists today in youth's awareness and discussion of sexual liberation. While antisexist clarification has begun to present itself, further clarification is needed.

The women's and gay movements have been instrumental in uncovering a good deal of the contradictions in sexuality. While the media were pushing the "sexual revolution," these movements began to speak of the oppressive power relationships in human sexuality and of how a political movement ought to transcend repressed sexuality as much as repressed political power. While Masters and Johnson (and related theorists) could only bring out technical aspects (orgasmic frequency, how to manipulate genitals, etc.), the women's and gay movements could bring out the fuller human potential, a step above simple "success." Success, in fact, enters into sexuality in much the same way as it arises from capitalism—economically, it is measured by what can be gained from the encounter; socially and culturally, by what can be proved by the encounter.

We also learned how sexuality in our society is male-oriented, power-oriented, mystified, supportive of conservative social relationships.[2] If one person treats another as a sex object, how can the two achieve any kind of social equality? The same object orientation would be a part of all other aspects of the person's life, and profit and power would triumph over pleasure and integration.

Sports, clothes, music, cars, games, etc., all reflect the dominant ethic of society, including the sexual ethic. Thus the man is powerful, athletic, potent, aggressive; the woman is submissive, docile, powerless. From the TV ads to the playing fields, a false sexuality is imprinted on people's minds. The sexual object is out there, a symbol of reality. We watch the athlete or singer, we "have" sex as we would a cigarette—from a distance that allows for no involvement on our parts and revolves around protectiveness, fear, and compartmentalization of our lives. Like the scientific observer, we remain detached because we have learned no other way. The new forms of communication, which could be liberating, reinforce the sexual repression of earlier days and bring the message into living rooms and bedrooms like Big Brother. Reich showed that sexually awakened youth would be far more dangerous to the ruling class than sexually repressed Communists would. Such youth would move from sexual liberation to other areas: they would become dissatisfied with bourgeois relations of work, family structure, government, and so forth. The ruling classes respond to sexual awakening both knowingly and unknowingly—in the nurseries, the kid shows on TV, etc.

Physicians and mental health professionals held on

2 An excellent article on this and other aspects of sexuality is Karen Rotkin's "The Phallacy of Our Sexual Norm," *Rough Times,* vol. 3, no. 1 (September 1972).

to the myth of the vaginal orgasm for a long time.[3] This was an attempt to preserve male dominance over women by restraining their sexual capacities and initiative—and thus the liberation of their energy in general. Now that the myth is shot, they get the sex "act" down to a series of maneuvers that replace human pleasure with technical expertise. The rash of sex manuals is one social answer to people's needs for a liberated sexuality. Their technicality must be the ultimate capitalist triumph over sexuality.

But such forms are not allowed everyone. Most people still live in fear of parents, police, and the devil. Young women still get sent to mental hospitals and jails for independent sexual expression. Homosexuals still get the most vicious treatment: long jail sentences, behavior modification (gay men in behavior modification programs are given electric shocks to their penises if they get erections from photos of naked men). It is obvious that these political attacks on sexual "maladjustment" are responses to political questions and not to psychological instincts. The state and the sexually repressed person are partners, and if the latter gets wise, the former loses.

THE SEXUAL SPECTACLE

The craziness of the sexual-political trends in our society is well expressed in the "swinger" movement. Swingers' group sex is a reflection of mass-technical culture. The alienated social relationships of daily life apparently are insoluble for swingers, so they enter into a realm of activities that are devoid of friendship

[3] A fine article is Anne Koedt's "The Myth of the Vaginal Orgasm," in *The Radical Therapist* (New York: Ballantine, 1972), pp. 127–139.

or warmth. Having no common interest save swinger parties, these people play at creating sexual contact. They don't succeed, in that their relationships reflect the same sexual code as has always existed. Swingers' sexuality is divorced from the rest of their lives and becomes sadomasochistic and voyeuristic (power-submission and nonattachment). What kind of failure in society can produce a mode of behavior so alien to its own nature? What quality of life is available that can so enslave sexuality and humanity?

Sexual submission and repressive desublimation create the form for alienated sexuality. This follows from the basic division of labor and the more specific forms of alienation of work and living which we encounter all the time. People with little or no power over any aspect of their lives can hardly enter into nonalienated sexual relationships. Sexual sublimation is an early phase of capitalist development, a phase of hoarding and accumulation. In the sexual sphere this becomes a hoarding and competitive sexuality. As capitalism develops to a technological system, it puts fewer checks on the overt expression of sexuality. Thus the consumerist aspects of modern capitalism create an advertised medium of gratification. Everything is held up to the camera for isolated contact; a spectacle is invented to dazzle, to tease, to lift you up and drop you down. The swingers are a type of sexual spectacle that presents society's technological humanity in a most repressive and alienated form.

The range of technology extends from pleasure stimulation by electronic brain control to *A Clockwork Orange* nightmares. There is adequate reason to suppose that the technicians of capitalism will extend their social control to the sexual sphere. Between electronic stimulation of the brain, swinger spectacles, technical sex manuals, and media trips of the gadget society, the human choices become clearer: liberation or enslavement.

SEXUAL INTEGRATION

Sexuality needs to be integrated with sensuality, human sensory awareness, communication between people. Sexual pleasure is not by nature isolated from other pleasures; social forces create the isolation. As Reich understood it, the repression of sexuality and politics was unified; thus the liberation of both would be a unified process. The struggle for sexual liberation cannot advance without the struggle for all liberation, and political liberation will have little meaning without sexual liberation. The two interact dialectically with each other to create a different mode of struggle and different forms of social relations among people.

The persecution of revolutionaries like Reich and Alexandra Kollontai[4] follows logically from the authoritarian socialists' fear of total liberation, as well as from a reaction to the social patterns of behavior that these revolutionaries tried to break down. When sexual boundaries are altered, it becomes clear that the entire social order is in question. The sexual struggle becomes an internal dynamic in the total process of revolution.

Integration is not an easy question. There can be no set patterns or instructions. Unlike the technology of bourgeois culture, liberated sexuality expresses the

[4] Alexandra Kollontai, "Sexual Relations and the Class Struggle" and "Love and the New Morality," pamphlet by Falling Wall Press, 79 Richmond Road, Montpelier, Bristol, England.

social being of people in union with their production, art, values, etc. We seek a society in which sexual pleasure will be related to all the things we do with our lives. Work, play, sexuality, and creativity are not forever separable. *We need a vision of their unity in order to begin struggling for that unity.*

Genital-oriented sexuality often obscures other sensual pleasure. People tend to be geared solely toward having an orgasm, and a genital one at that. Their sexual desires and responses are reflections of this. The concept of foreplay feeds this false genitality. Touching and caressing a lover's body is seen as "preparatory." Preparatory to what? If it is your lover's body, nothing is "preparatory." A result of this genitality is a great amount of detachment from the overall pleasure of sexual encounter, since the techniques involved require rational thinking-out rather than flowing with the person involved.

We need to explore all parts of the body and to understand that pleasurable feelings can be found in many ways. The fact that we deal in "types" of sex is indicative of our lack of integration. Oral sex is differentiated from genital sex, etc., and the result is a one-or-the-other attitude that lowers the level of sensuality. People don't usually talk to their lovers about what they would like to do sexually, what part of their body tingles and when. We shut up for fear of being "uncool" and therefore wind up frustrated or angry. Real contact could mean a deeper knowledge and communication with the other person. But the privitization of our lives doesn't allow for such contact. We have separated sexuality from the rest of our lives to the point where we have different worlds for sex and nonsex.

We also don't look, or at least we don't look appreciatively, lovingly. Such looking has been conditioned out of us to prevent us from real participation. Thus we remain voyeurs of a sort. We cut off other human senses to partake of one in particular; the loss is of all senses. We make love at night so we can go to sleep afterward. Why don't we make love at other times, too—at the beginning of the day, or in the middle of one—and learn to let things wait to be done a little later? Of course, this is a real difficulty, given most people's work schedules and problems with child care and the like. One approach would be to formulate demands for the restructuring of work to make possible a realization of such alternative actions.

While sexuality will be no freer than any other aspect of life in bourgeois society until that society ends, we can begin to struggle at present with new ways of living. If we don't, the struggle will be incomplete. Sexual politics need to be voiced and acted on so that they can be integrated into the movement that is transforming the world.

9. Dare to Struggle, Dare to Win!

I hope that the sequence of this book has seemed as logical to you as it has to me. When one is synthesizing a new way of looking at things, it is not perfectly clear how to proceed. In my collection, *Radical Psychology*, I felt it necessary to present articles and excerpts from those people who were influences in the formation of a radical psychology. With more clarification and practical work, I then felt it necessary to tie together those influences into the beginnings of a theory of Marxist psychology. As I have written this book, its major impact on me has been to bring me to the realization that *a Marxist psychology is only a partial aspect of a Marxist world view.*

One does not simply adopt a new world view, a total conceptual framework within which to view the world. Even to use the term "world view" can lead to confusion. Nevertheless, revolutionary change is bound to create a new world view that will replace the traditional ways of looking at the world. With a grasp of Marxism, aspects of reality open up that never before seemed to exist. It is a process of uncovering. What I wish to do here is to present a broad perspective of what such a world view does. This is integrally related to a politically revolutionary struggle in that the revolution is a revolution of all human-social relations. It is necessary to realize that the new world view is but one aspect of the unity of political struggle in creating a new world.

The society in which we live is a class society—capitalists and their technicians rule over the majority of others, who work for them in various ways. Capital buys labor power and makes profit from that labor power. In the process human relations are changed as manifestations of the economic base. For instance, in feudalism all members of the family worked together; capitalism divided labor by having the man as the wage slave and the woman as the domestic producer of work and also as the reproducer of the family. The nuclear family not only guarantees this separation but also socializes the child into the correct role. As Reich showed, the pattern of authoritarian control by the father conditions the child to filial obedience, sexual sublimation, and faithfulness to the state. The woman and children are objects of the man in the same way that the man's labor power is an object of the capitalist. As the ethic of competition entered into capitalist production, so too did it enter into family reproduction. Jealousy became an economic reaction, as did much of the behavior that psychologists tend to call instinctual. Profit and loss in business were translated into similar attitudes in interpersonal encounter.

As an example of this, one can look back to the end of the antipsychiatry chapter, where Esterson's analysis of Sarah Danzig's family situation shows us the direct relation between financial and familial capitalism. Sarah was seen by her father as an investment, much as he would view his inventory. We can also look at television and see our sexuality, robbed from us initially, being sold back to us as commodities. Even on the less direct levels the same phenomenon takes place: we view friendships as exchanges of favors, patterns of getting and giving based on an economic ideal rather than a communal ideal. In this economic ideal people are atomized individuals, fighting for survival. For the ruling class the fight for survival is among the masses of people; for the revolutionary forces the fight is between them and the rulers.

The difference is vast. As Fanon shows, oppressed people find it easier, for lack of alternative visions, to kill each other rather than the oppressors. This is not a simple mechanism but a long-unfolding pattern by which people come to see themselves as having their own problems, caused instinctually rather than socially. Thus a child who is unhappy in school is compelled to accept his unfortunate "learning disability" instead of helped to understand fully his passive role in the education process; a child is made to feel guilty for disobeying a parent although he apparently knows that the parental order is detrimental to his being. At each point, the capitalist order forces *internalization* of the problem.

A total revolution *externalizes* the problems in that it finds the social reasons for the "problems" and social answers to them. Thus sexual repression is combatted not by moralism but by conscious action aimed at sexual liberation. We don't fight the church or the state on philosophical levels; the philosophical levels are part of the political levels of struggle. This is not to say that revolutionary ideology does not enter into the struggle; it is integral to it but in dialectical unity with action. Further theory comes out of expanded practice, and further practice comes out of expanded theory. Thus if a popular struggle against anticontraceptive legislation takes place, it cannot be based solely on ideas. Those engaged in such an effort would need to concentrate also on the personally and collectively liberating aspects of free contraception on demand. Workers taking over a factory go from simple occupation to use of the facilities for revolutionary activities.

In the process of political struggle the relations between people change. We learn to see a neighbor or coworker as an ally, not a competitor; we learn to see that power comes through unity and that collective effort leads to expanded individual freedom. We learn that things are not by nature "conservative" or "radical." For instance, conservative education is supposedly a system in which student initiative is limited and discipline arbitrarily enforced; radical education is seen as a noncoercive process of example, emulation, and support. How can these two things possibly both be "education?" In fact, the "conservative" educator is training the student for a life in capitalist society, and the "radical" educator is helping the student to fight that society and create a new one. Thus we have political struggle, class struggle, rather than different "types" of education. So, too, for all aspects of our lives—the psychology, engineering, food-packaging, arts, etc.,—of the society in which we live reflect their class origins, not their "pure" forms.

By extension one cannot plug "radical" concepts into "conservative" methods. An example of this is the propensity of various leftist psychologists to insist that behavior modification can be used for social change if the "right" values are reinforced. Such people do not understand that the method of behavior modification is itself a method based on the prevailing values of our society: that a wise professional can instill the correct values in the errant person. That attitude arises out of psychology, not out of liberation—by which I mean the actual differences, in practice, between the two opposed world views. Psychology is one reflection of the bourgeois mode of thought and is fundamentally opposed to the liberating mode. Ultimately this takes the form of academic arguments among the professionals who decide on what the people need. This is their social function, not their "pure" attitude. The existence of professionals/technicians has a material base. The lawyer protects the institution of private property, the psychologist and psychiatrist protect the institution of social propriety, the physician protects the institution of regulated illness and death, and so on. It is the nature of the system that such functions continue.

Since it is the nature of the system, we cannot expect some miraculous change in the ideology of such people. Rather, we need action based on material forces. Some of this has begun: the attack of women's liberation and mental patients' liberation on psychiatry has caused many others to join in that attack, and the result is that many people think twice before going to a therapist. In many other areas of society people have begun to take control of their lives. The Wounded Knee occupation by the Oglala Sioux, for instance, is a major event of our times by which we can learn how oppressed people take back the natural power of which they have been robbed. It results in solidarity, kinship, and loving support; it creates new ways of relating. And so on with all political struggles

—they alter the nature of human relations, since they change the reins of power from the rule by a few to the living together of all.

It is clear that the process of revolution has many appearances to many people. For some it is a threat to their security even if they don't have much to start with. For others it is a threat to their personal power—such as adults fearing children's liberation. For some people revolution is an exciting process in which their lives change in more ways than they can realize, and they revel in the joy of it. This is close to the idea I am trying to convey: that revolution is a turning about of all the ways we have learned to live and a joyous process of uncovering human possibilities that were unknown before.

It is no accident that the revolutionary movement in this country has thrown forward cultural forms of expression and sexual forms of liberation. The struggle for sexual integration and for creative culture are part of the same unity that includes workers' control at the point of production. The types of culture that arise out of revolutionary struggles are types that reflect the material realities of the struggle. Marge Piercy writes: "We are trying to live/as if we were an experiment/conducted by the future,/blasting the walls of the cells/that no protective device or inhibition/has evolved to replace."[1]

We are in the midst of evolving a type of human existence with different a priori definitions. Psychology, like the ruling-class forms of production/distribution that it supports, believes in a pessimistic humanity for which "original sin," "instinct," or "in-

[1] Marge Piercy, "Rough Times," *Rough Times,* vol. 3, no. 4 (February–March 1973).

appropriate response" dictate the need for social control. Marxism counters such an attitude with its own view of humanity: humanity struggling to achieve unity with nature and human activity, transcending the past in the creation of newness. Marxism is a reflection of the present struggles, not merely another ideology. Thus *it mirrors the human social activity* that is involved in the revolutionary process. Instead of passive pawns, we become active creators.

Marxism can approach psychology in the sense that the thought and behavior of people changes drastically in communist society. With people controlling the process of their work, they are at unity with their creation rather than providing labor power for others. With people controlling the distribution of social wealth (all that is produced by social beings), they are at unity with others in their world, since the distribution is based on need, not profit. In the struggle for a communist society, culture (in its broadest sense) becomes integrated with work. The division of labor will be abolished, and we will no longer be cogs in a machine. Children will cease to be isolated from the daily life of their parents, since their parents will no longer be their only source of support, physical or emotional. When art, music, sexuality, comradeship, work, and everything else are separated from the nexus of exchange value and profit, people will view these things differently and begin to take part in them.

In this sense the realization of a new world based on the insights of Marxism creates new psychic forces. Thus Marxism can approach this new psychology. But by itself neither psychology nor political struggle can reflect a wholeness. These categories will break down, as will other categories that serve to separate the mind from the body from the spirit. *When people compre-*

hend the world differently, it is because that world is changing and they play a part in that change.

What forms will this take? That is the most common question posed in response to an analysis such as I have presented here. One answer is that it will take *all* forms, since all forms will change. That may be a simplistic answer, especially in the absence for most people yet of revolutionary changes; however, specifics may not be totally understandable, particularly when they relate to some people and not to others. This is the early stage of the transformation, when struggles in one sector are not integrated with struggles in another sector. But the intregration is taking place. Workers' organizations, mass organizations against imperialism, the women's movement, mental patients' liberation, and prison organizing may seem disparate now, but they are coming together. This coming together means more than simply the recognition of common goals; it means that each area of struggle learns from the others, expanding its own nature.

On the most personal level, the revolution is a transformation of the way we live, think, act. Integrating ourselves with our world implies our daily involvement with, and pleasure in, what we do in all areas. The new psyche will reflect the world in ways fundamentally different from those of the present psyche, since the world will be different. Being alone will become being-with-oneself, being in a group will become being-with-others; the social realm of existence will be altered and in turn will enhance the individual experience of the world.

None of this comes easy, since those in power are not about to concede anything other than what they want to concede. Creating alternate institutions works only insofar as those alternatives are not crushed by the ruling class. When they are crushed (e.g., Mayor Daley's closing of people's day-care centers, the Los Angeles police busting a women's clinic), the alternative institution becomes a form of struggle. Similarly, individual actions, or what we think are individual actions (for instance, engaging in liberated sexuality may seem individual but is in fact a social event), lead to social conflict and to the escalation of struggle.

To engage in any struggle for freedom means to come in conflict with those who restrict our freedom. Additionally, it means understanding the contradictions between people, since most people have internalized the ruling ideology. So it becomes necessary to create modes of struggle that offer real changes to those people in order to break down the internalized oppression that keeps them in one or another form of slavery. Without glorifying violence, we must be aware that armed struggle is ultimately necessary.

In this effort revolutionaries in the area of self-help, radical psychology will contribute their own perspectives, which will alter other perspectives, and their own perspectives will in turn be altered. The slogan, "Mental health is revolution. Revolution is mental health," implies the transcendence of "mental health" as an archaic classification made by bourgeois society. It further implies that psychic fullness and human freedom come about only as an integrated part of total communist revolution—when those who produce wealth control that wealth.

There is essentially only one fight. Vietnam, Palestine, Orangeburg, Lordstown, national struggles within this country, workers' struggles, women's struggles, mental patients' struggles, and all others are building to the worldwide revolution that will erase from human existence the paralyzing forces that have governed it so far. In this, *Marxist psychology can offer a view of the integral relationship between the psyche and the material world and attempt to end the distinction between them.*

Bibliography

This list is not complete in that all books of an author are not necessarily included. A number of books might not be considered "radical" but are nevertheless important in the development of a Marxist psychology. *Rough Times* (formerly *The Radical Therapist*) is recommended for current reading. The best articles from the magazine's first two years appear in collections, respectively titled *The Radical Therapist* and *Rough Times* (New York: Ballantine, 1972 and 1973).

GENERAL AND SOCIOLOGICAL

Baritz, Loren. *The Servants of Power.* Middletown, Conn.: Wesleyan University Press, 1960.

Brown, Phil, ed. *Radical Psychology.* New York: Harper & Row, 1973.

Clark, Ted, and Jaffe, Dennis. *Toward a Radical Therapy.* New York: Gordon & Breach, 1973.

Ennis, Bruce. *Prisoners of Psychiatry*. New York: Harcourt Brace Jovanovich, 1972.

Foucault, Michel. *Madness and Civilization*. Translated by Richard Howard. New York: Pantheon, 1965.

Friedman, Neil. *The Social Nature of Psychological Research*. New York: Basic Books, 1967.

Glenn, Michael and Richard Kunnes. *Repression or Revolution?: Therapy in the United States Today*. New York: Harper & Row, 1973.

Goffman, Erving. *Asylums*. Chicago: Aldine, 1961.

————. *Behavior in Public Places*. New York: Free Press, 1963.

————. *Interaction Ritual*. Chicago: Aldine, 1967.

————. *The Presentation of Self in Everyday Life*. New York: Doubleday, 1959.

————. *Relations in Public*. New York: Basic Books, 1971.

————. *Stigma*. Englewood Cliffs, N.J.: Prentice-Hall, 1963.

Hollingshead, A. B., and Redlich, F. C. *Social Class and Mental Illness*. New York: John Wiley, 1958.

Lynd, Helen M. *On Shame and the Search for Identity*. New York: Harcourt Brace Jovanovich, 1958.

Rosen, George. *Madness in Society*. New York: Harper & Row, 1967.

Scheff, Thomas J. *Being Mentally Ill*. Chicago: Aldine, 1966.

————, ed. *Mental Illness and Social Processes*. New York: Harper & Row, 1967.

Szasz, Thomas S. *The Age of Madness*. New York: Doubleday, 1973.

————. *Ideology and Insanity*. New York: Doubleday, 1970.

――――. *Law, Liberty, and Psychiatry*. New York: Macmillan, 1963.

――――. *The Manufacture of Madness*. New York: Harper & Row, 1970.

――――. *The Myth of Mental Illness*. New York: Harper & Row, 1961.

ANTIPSYCHIATRY

Barnes, Mary, and Berke, Joe. *Mary Barnes: Two Accounts of a Journey through Madness*. New York: Harcourt Brace Jovanovich, 1972.

Berke, Joe, ed. *Counter-Culture*. New York: Hillary House, 1971.

Cooper, David. *The Death of the Family*. New York: Pantheon, 1970.

――――. *Psychiatry and Anti-Psychiatry*. New York: Ballantine, 1967.

――――, ed. *To Free a Generation*. New York: Macmillan, 1969.

Esterson, Aaron. *The Leaves of Spring*. London: Tavistock, 1971.

Laing, R. D. *The Divided Self*. New York: Pantheon, 1970.

――――. *Knots*. New York: Pantheon, 1970.

――――. *The Politics of Experience*. New York: Pantheon, 1967.

――――. *The Politics of the Family*. New York: Pantheon, 1969.

――――. *The Self and Others*. New York: Pantheon, 1970.

Laing, R. D., and Cooper, David. *Reason and Violence*. New York: Barnes & Noble, 1964.

Laing, R. D., and Esterson, Aaron. *Sanity, Madness*

and the Family. 2d ed. New York: Basic Books, 1971.

Laing, R. D., Phillipson, H., and Lee, A. R. *Interpersonal Perception.* New York: Springer, 1966.

Schatzman, Morton. *Soul Murder.* New York: Pantheon, 1973.

LEFT FREUDIANS

Brown, Bruce. *Marx, Freud, and the Critique of Everyday Life.* New York: Monthly Review Press, 1973.

Cattier, Michel. *The Life and Work of Wilhelm Reich.* New York: Horizon, 1972.

Fromm, Erich. *Beyond the Chains of Illusion: My Encounter with Marx and Freud.* New York: Simon & Schuster, 1967.

————. *Escape from Freedom.* New York: Holt, 1941.

————. *The Revolution of Hope: Toward a Humanized Technology.* New York: Harper & Row, 1970.

————. *The Sane Society.* New York: Holt, 1955.

Marcuse, Herbert. *Eros and Civilization: A Philosophical Inquiry into Freud.* Boston: Beacon Press, 1955.

————. *An Essay on Liberation.* Boston: Beacon Press, 1969.

————. *Five Lectures.* Translated by Jeremy Shapiro and Sherry Weber. Boston: Beacon Press, 1970.

————. *One-Dimensional Man: Studies in the Ideology of Advanced Industrial Society.* Boston: Beacon Press, 1964.

Reich, Wilhelm. *Character Analysis.* Translated by Vincent Carfagno. New York: Farrar, Straus & Company, 1949.

————. *The Function of the Orgasm.* New York: Farrar, Straus & Cudahy, 1961.

————. *The Invasion of Compulsory Sex-Morality.* New York: Farrar, Straus & Giroux, 1971.

————. *The Mass Psychology of Fascism.* Translated by Vincent Carfagno. New York: Farrar, Straus & Giroux, 1970.

————. *Selected Sex-Pol Essays, 1934–37.* London: Socialist Reproduction, 1973. 57d Jamestown Road, London NW1 ($2).

————. *Sex-Pol.* Edited by Lee Baxandall. New York: Random House, 1972.

————. *The Sexual Revolution.* New York: Farrar, Straus & Giroux, 1963.

————. *The Sexual Struggle of Youth.* London: Socialist Reproduction, 1973. ($1.75)

————. "What Is Class Consciousness?" *Liberation,* October 1971.

Reiche, Reimut. *Sexuality and Class Struggle.* London: New Left Books, 1971.

Robinson, Paul A. *The Freudian Left: Wilhelm Reich, Géza Róheim, Herbert Marcuse.* New York: Harper & Row, 1969.

THE MARXIST FOUNDATION

Engels, Friedrich. *The Origin of the Family, Private Property, and the State.* New York: International Publishers, 1972.

Fanon, Frantz. *Black Skin, White Masks.* Translated by Charles L. Markmann. New York: Grove Press, 1967.

————. *A Dying Colonialism.* Translated by Haakon Chevalier. New York: Grove Press, 1967.

————. *Toward the African Revolution*. New York: Grove Press, 1968.

————. *The Wretched of the Earth*. Translated by Constance Farrington. New York: Grove Press, 1965.

Gramsci, Antonio. *The Modern Prince and Other Writings*. New York: International Publishers, 1959.

————. *Prison Notebooks*. New York: International Publishers, 1959.

Kollontai, Alexandra. *Communism and the Family*. London: Pluto Press, 1972.

————. *Sexual Relations and the Class Struggle*. Translated by Alix Holt. London: Falling Wall Press, 1972.

Luxemburg, Rosa. *The Mass Strike*. New York: Harper & Row, 1971.

————. *Rosa Luxemburg Speaks*. New York: Pathfinder Press, 1970.

Mao Tse-tung. "Combat Liberalism." In *Five Articles*. New York: China Books.

————. *Four Essays on Philosophy*. New York: China Books, 1968.

————. *The Investigation into Peasant Movement in Hunan*. New York: China Books.

Marx, Karl. *The Communist Manifesto*.

————. *Economic and Philosophic Manuscripts of 1844*. Edited by Dirk J. Struik, translated by Martin Milligan. New York: International Publishers, 1964.

————. *The Eighteenth Brumaire of Louis Bona-Parte*. New York: International Publishers, 1963.

————. *The Grundrisse* (abridged). Edited and translated by David McLellan. New York: Harper & Row, 1970.

———. *The Grundrisse* (complete). Translated by Martin Nicolaus. London: Penguin, 1973.

———. *The Poverty of Philosophy*. New York: International Publishers, 1963.

———. *Wages, Price and Profit*. New York: China Books, 1965.

———, and Engels, Friedrich. *The German Ideology*. New York: International Publishers, 1970.

RACISM

Cleaver, Eldridge. *Post-Prison Writing and Speeches*. New York: Random House, 1969.

———. *Soul on Ice*. New York: McGraw-Hill, 1968.

Davis, Angela. *If They Come in the Morning*. Third Press, 1971.

Ellison, Ralph. *Invisible Man*. New York: Random House, 1952.

Hernton, Calvin. *Sex and Racism in America*. New York: Grove Press, 1966.

Jackson, George. *Blood in My Eye*. New York: Random House, 1972.

———. *Soledad Brother*. New York: Coward, 1971.

Malcolm X. *Autobiography of Malcolm X*. New York: Grove Press, 1966.

———. *Malcolm X Speaks*. New York: Merit Publishers.

Mann, Eric. *Comrade George*. New York: Harper & Row, 1974.

Thomas, Alexander, and Sillen, Samuel. *Racism and Psychiatry*. New York: Brunner-Mazel, 1972.

SEX ROLES

Altbach, Edith, ed. *From Feminism to Liberation*. Cambridge, Mass.: Schenkman, 1971.

Babcox, Deborah, and Belkin, Madeline. *Liberation Now!*

Beauvoir, Simone de. *The Second Sex*. Translated by H. M. Parshley. New York: Knopf, 1953.

Chesler, Phyllis. *Women and Madness*. New York: Doubleday, 1972.

Come Out! Washington, N.J.: Times Change Press.

Firestone, Shulamith. *The Dialectic of Sex*. New York: Morrow, 1970.

Garskoff, Michelle, ed. *Roles Women Play*. Belmont, Calif.: Brooks Cole, 1971.

Millett, Kate. *Sexual Politics*. New York: Doubleday, 1970.

Mitchell, Juliet. *Women's Estate*. New York: Pantheon, 1971.

Rowbotham, Sheila. *Women, Resistance & Revolution*. New York: Vintage, 1974.

Roszak, Betty, and Roszak, Theodore, eds. *Masculine/Feminine*. New York: Harper & Row, 1969.

Sherman, Julia. *On the Psychology of Women*. Chicago: Charles C. Thomas, 1971.

EXISTENTIAL/PHENOMENOLOGICAL PSYCHOLOGY

Binswanger, Ludwig. *Being-in-the-World*. Translated by Jacob Needleman. New York: Basic Books, 1963.

May, Rollo, et al., eds. *Existence*. New York: Basic Books, 1958.

Merleau-Ponty, Maurice. *The Primacy of Perception*. Evanston, Ill.: Northwestern University Press, 1964.
———. *The Structure of Behavior*. Boston: Beacon Press, 1963.

Ruitenbeek, Hendrik M., ed. *Psychoanalysis and Existential Philosophy*. New York: Dutton, 1962.

Sartre, Jean-Paul. *Existential Psychoanalysis*. Chicago: Regnery, 1962.

————. *Search for a Method*. Translated by Hazel E. Barnes. New York: Knopf, 1963.

Van Kaam, Adrian. *Existential Foundations of Psychology*. Pittsburgh: Duquesne University Press, 1966.

FICTION

Green, Hannah. *I Never Promised You a Rose Garden*. New York: Holt, 1964.

Kesey, Ken. *One Flew over the Cuckoo's Nest*. New York: Viking Press, 1962.

Keyes, Daniel. *Flowers for Algernon*. New York: Harcourt Brace Jovanovich, 1966.

Lessing, Doris. *Briefing for a Descent into Hell*. New York: Knopf, 1971.

————. *The Golden Notebook*. New York: Simon & Schuster, 1962.

Plath, Sylvia. *The Bell Jar*. New York: Harper & Row, 1971.

Wheelis, Allen. *The Illusionless Man*. New York: Harper & Row, 1971.

NEW WAYS OF LIVING

Hinton, William. *Fanshen: A Documentary of Revolution in a Chinese Village*. New York: Monthly Review Press, 1967.

Horn, Joshua. *Away with All Pests*. New York: Monthly Review Press, 1971.

Negrin, Su. *Begin at Start*. Washington, N.J.: Times Change Press, 1972.

Index